LAWYERS in MODERN CHINA

LAWYERS in MODERN CHINA

Richard Komaiko
and Beibei Que

CAMBRIA PRESS

AMHERST, NEW YORK

Copyright 2009 Richard Komaiko and Beibei Que

All rights reserved
Printed in the United States of America

No part of this publication may be reproduced, stored in or introduced into a retrieval system, or transmitted, in any form, or by any means (electronic, mechanical, photocopying, recording, or otherwise), without the prior permission of the publisher.

Requests for permission should be directed to:
permissions@cambriapress.com, or mailed to:
Cambria Press
20 Northpointe Parkway, Suite 188
Amherst, NY 14228

Library of Congress Cataloging-in-Publication Data

Komaiko, Richard.
   Lawyers in modern China / Richard Komaiko & Beibei Que.
      p. cm.
   Includes bibliographical references and index.
   ISBN 978-1-60497-648-9 (alk. paper)
 1. Lawyers—China. 2. Practice of law—China. 3. Lawyers—United States.
I. Que, Beibei. II. Title.

   KNQ1630.K66 2009
   340.023'51—dc22

2009034790

*To Mr. Si Weijiang, whose idealism and
independent thought inspire all those around him*

TABLE OF CONTENTS

List of Figures	ix
Foreword	xi
Introduction: Frustration	1
Chapter 1: The Role of Lawyer	7
Chapter 2: Cultural Background	15
Chapter 3: The Rule of Law	53
Chapter 4: Becoming a Chinese Lawyer	91
Chapter 5: A Day in the Life	109
Chapter 6: Frustrations in the Practice of Law	121
Chapter 7: The Market for Chinese Lawyers	133
Chapter 8: Policy Recommendations	151
Conclusion: Beyond the Mandate of Heaven	159
Appendices	**163**
A. Chinese Law Schools	163
B. Chinese Terms	171
C. Sample Interview Questions	173
Notes	**177**

Bibliography	191
Index	205
About the Authors	209

List of Figures

Figure 1.	King George III and George Washington.	22
Figure 2.	Italian Jesuit Matteo Ricci preaching in Beijing, circa 1600.	26
Figure 3.	CPSC recalls by country since 2001.	63
Figure 4.	Screen shot of Facebook.	66
Figure 5.	Screen shot of Xiaonei.	67
Figure 6.	Trends in piracy experienced by American companies in China.	68
Figure 7.	China's anticounterfeiting bureaucracy.	72
Figure 8.	Number of laws and administrative regulations in comparison.	77
Figure 9.	Length of Chinese constitutions as a function of time.	78
Figure 10.	Length of Chinese patent and trademark laws as a function of time.	79
Figure 11.	Number of Chinese billionaires as a function of time.	86

Figure 12.	Top ten law schools in China.	96
Figure 13.	*The Declaration of Independence* at People's University Law School.	98
Figure 14.	*Judgment of Solomon* at People's University Law School.	99
Figure 15.	*Papinionous* at People's University Law School.	100
Figure 16.	Recent administrations of the Unified Judicial Examination.	104
Figure 17.	Inverted pyramid of mandatory authority in the Chinese legal system.	124
Figure 18.	Lawyer populations in absolute terms.	136
Figure 19.	Lawyer populations per thousand citizens.	137
Figure 20.	Lawyer populations per US$100 million of gross domestic product.	138
Figure 21.	Income of Shanghai lawyers under thirty years old.	141

Foreword

This volume represents the efforts of two of my former students, one a lawyer and the other an economist, who shared an interest in the Chinese legal system. Armed with their prodigious intellectual curiosity, they set out to understand the situation of Chinese lawyers. They designed an extensive program of research and interviewed dozens of lawyers, first in the United States and then in various locations around China. The result is a fresh look at a phenomenon of great importance to China's future.

China's rapid economic development has generated great demand for legal services, and law has gained status as a field of study. Tens of thousands of students begin legal studies each year, and the profession has expanded rapidly. At the same time that the number of lawyers has increased, the role of lawyers is changing, as is the nature of practice, in response to an evolving and continuously more sophisticated regulatory and market environment. Keeping up with all the changes is difficult for anyone not living in the middle of it, and even a challenge for those who are.

The paradoxes of the socialist rule of law are many. Few governments have conducted such a comprehensive program of law reform as China has, but implementation of law is often mired in localism and personalism. The rule of law promotes order and certainty, but there are clear limits to either in a society undergoing such rapid change. It promises that none should be above the law, but this is difficult to implement in a one-party state. At the same time, citizens regularly win administrative lawsuits against the government, and courts are increasingly the locus of litigation implicating major social and economic issues. Law is important to understand outcomes.

Lawyers in China must navigate their way among the rule-of-law ideal, the logic of the party-state, and a rapidly shifting market for services. The legal profession thus exhibits all of the dynamism of China today, while facing particular challenges. Some lawyers attempt to use law to effect social change. Others focus on keeping up with the business environment. In any field they work in, lawyers are pushing the boundaries every day in today's China.

This book traces the development of the rule of law with Chinese characteristics and provides a comprehensive snapshot of the situation of Chinese lawyers today. It will be of great value to those seeking to understand how and why China's lawyers have come to their current position, while also providing clues as to how things may develop in the future. This study arrives at a landmark time, as 2009 is the thirtieth anniversary of the revival of the legal profession in China. The authors are to be congratulated for their spirit of empirical inquiry, and their careful efforts are well worth your while.

—Tom Ginsburg
University of Chicago Law School

LAWYERS in MODERN CHINA

INTRODUCTION

FRUSTRATION

In the advent of the 2008 Summer Olympics, the Chinese government made repeated promises that it would allow peaceful protests to occur in Beijing. Following on this promise, three public parks, colloquially referred to as "protest pens," were demarcated for hosting protests. Individuals interested in protesting were instructed to file a formal application with the Beijing Municipal Public Security Bureau. According to the New China News Agency, seventy-seven applications were received, but not a single application was approved.[1] The Beijing Organizing Committee for the Olympic Games explained away the lack of approvals by asserting that all of the grievances had been resolved privately.[2] Not only is it untrue that the grievances were resolved privately, but many people were actually punished for submitting applications in accordance with the government's own instructions! Ms. Wu Dianyuan, age seventy-nine, and Ms. Wang Xiuying, age seventy-seven, were both sentenced to one year of labor camp reeducation for submitting applications to protest their forced evictions from their homes in 2001.[3] Many people felt a disturbing sense of frustration owing to the government's failure to uphold its promise, and an even greater sense of frustration owing to the government's empty assertion that it *had* upheld its promise. This experience demonstrated on a grand scale one of the most vexing problems in China today: promises are made casually and broken frequently, which causes great frustration.

This problem is manifested not only at the macroscopic level, such as with the Olympic protest scandal, but also at the microscopic level. A small business firm will make a promise about the quality of a product to a client. When the promise is broken and a shoddy product is delivered, the client is left holding the bag. It is unclear whether the promise was broken because the firm did not possess the ability to keep the promise or because the firm did not possess the intention to keep the promise. Either way, the client becomes extremely frustrated. What are his options for redress? Who can he turn to in order to compel the firm to fulfill its promise? How can he pursue future business opportunities if he cannot trust that commercial promises will be fulfilled?

There are no simple answers to these questions, nor are there easy means of dispelling the clouds of frustration that hover above China today. Westerners may be inclined to dismiss these as Chinese problems. But, in fact, they are global problems. Imagine that tomorrow morning you pass a newsstand on the way to work. As soon as you see the newspaper, the headline jumps off the page: "World Unites Against Climate Change." You go on to read that the United Nations Framework Convention on Climate Change has finally broken through the gridlock; the nations of the world have united and agreed upon an equitable strategy for fighting climate change. The provisions have been worked out, the signatures have been applied, and the ink has dried. As the euphoria dies down, emissaries are sent all around the world. The emissaries explain how each country is to play its part, what regulations will be required, and what activities will be prohibited. Assuming that all countries intend to cooperate fully, we must ask, will the government of China be capable of holding up its end of the bargain? If it cannot enforce laws that were *made in China* and tailored to the contours of the Chinese polity, how will it be able to enforce one-size-fits-all laws that were imported from abroad? Will it be able to enforce the new regulations which will, undoubtedly, often run contrary to the directives of the market? If not, how effective can the agreement be? The agreement will surely collapse under the artificially heavy weight of the burden placed on the remaining states, to say nothing of the outrage that will justifiably follow the realization that the world's largest emitter of greenhouse gasses is not contributing any improvement. From this perspective, it is evident that China's frustrations are a matter of global relevance.

This book is a modest attempt to understand the frustration of China, as well as the uncertainty, disorder, and lack of accountability that lie at its root. The authors believe that these phenomena are best understood by examining Chinese lawyers. Lawyers are traffickers of certainty. Lawyers are wellsprings of order. Lawyers are bastions of accountability. If these three features are underrepresented in Chinese society, then the best way to understand their absence is to examine the group of people that is responsible, in most other societies, for their creation.

With these thoughts in mind, we engaged in a year-long research project designed to investigate and analyze Chinese lawyers. The first stage of research involved reading all of the prior literature on the topic, both in English and Chinese. Unfortunately, the topic of Chinese lawyers in general, and the relationship between Chinese lawyers and the weakness of the rule of law within China in particular, has been given inadequate attention by the academe. Max Weber's assertion that there were no lawyers in traditional Chinese society because there was no law in traditional Chinese society has largely been discredited as Orientalism appropriate only to its era.[4] Moreover, from the perspective of Professor H. L. A Hart's conception of law as an amalgam of primary and secondary rules, it may be argued that the social order that characterized traditional China was more befitting of the appellation *law* than the social order that characterizes modern China, for, as this work will explain, in traditional China there existed a generally accepted rule for identifying which rules should be followed, which cannot be said with any uniformity of modern China.

Professor Ethan Michelson has written a deeply informative doctoral dissertation which traces the development of the Chinese bar since the reforms of 1978.[5] The attention of the thesis, however, is focused on the sociology of the lawyers, rather than on their relationship to law or the rule of law.

A recurrent theme in the writings of Professor William Alford is a warning to beware of the dangerous assumption of universal convergence: the fact that American jurisprudence has evolved to rest upon certain pillars in no way limits the range of evolutionary paths open to Chinese jurisprudence.[6] Professor Randall Peerenboom has echoed this sentiment by observing that China may affect a rule-of-law system that is limited to formal legality without incorporating the substantive concepts that Westerners often assume to be indispensable.[7] These observations and warnings follow on the legacy of two generations of Sinologists that have fixated rather myopically on the role of the Communist Party, often to nonproductive ends. It has been posited that this is caused by the problem of access: a scholar cannot study what he cannot access, so when access is obstructed, all objects of study are viewed as mere instrumentalities which may possess the potential to dislodge the impediment. And so it is with the scholar's view of Chinese lawyers vis-à-vis the Communist Party. The overwhelming majority of Western analysis of the Chinese legal profession has viewed the bar as nothing more than a potential counterweight to the Communist Party. Professor Yves Dezalay has written that "law may begin to rival Communism—perhaps more precisely, the legal profession may rival the Party—as the leading legitimating authority."[8] Even Minxin Pei has written that legality may function as a "backdoor" through which gradual democratization could supplant the power of the party.[9] Not only are these outcomes unlikely, they miss the larger picture.

The second stage of research for this book involved traveling around the United States to interview Chinese lawyers who had come to America to do advanced legal training at American universities and firms. These interviews provided the authors with exposure to lawyers with an international and comparative perspective.

The final stage of research involved traveling around the People's Republic of China to interview Chinese lawyers. These interviews provided the authors with exposure to lawyers with a thoroughly domestic perspective. All together, hundreds of hours of interviews were conducted with more than sixty Chinese lawyers, law students, law professors, judges, clerks, government officials, and relevant experts from the nongovernmental organization (NGO) community in Beijing, Shanghai, Wuxi, Nanjing, New York, Washington, Los Angeles, and Chicago. All interviews were conducted under a strict promise of anonymity (unless otherwise arranged). In order to protect the identity of interview subjects, we shall not cite them by name but rather by a numeric code. A general template of interview questions is provided in the appendix. The interviews that were conducted in China, combined with the interviews that were conducted in America and the background research, have yielded a deep understanding of Chinese lawyers and their centrality to China's current situation. The aim of this book is to convey that understanding in an engaging and useful format.

The book begins with a general explanation of the legal profession in chapter 1. The second chapter offers a brief history of China. Although the history focuses on law and lawyers, it also sets their development against the context of the broader trends of politics and economics. The third chapter offers an explanation of the concept of the rule of law, what it means, how it is created, and its present status in China. The fourth chapter offers a primer on law school in China, including descriptions of the standard curriculum, the top schools, preparation for the bar exam, and entry into the field. The fifth chapter provides a series of anecdotes that illustrate some of the more salient features of the daily life of Chinese lawyers. The sixth chapter catalogues the most frustrating aspects of practicing law in China. The seventh chapter presents an analysis of the market for Chinese lawyers, including information about supply, demand, and the barriers that exist to a functioning market. The eighth chapter offers a brief series of policy recommendations that are designed to help strengthen the lawyer system and the rule of law. Finally, all of these themes are sewn together in the conclusion to explain the central argument of the book: the development of the Chinese legal profession is a consequence, rather than a cause, of political competition and societal openness. That Western dreams of employing the Chinese bar to instigate reform should be relinquished is not to say that Western interest in the Chinese bar should be abandoned. The Chinese bar is of paramount importance to Western observers *specifically* because it is a consequence rather than a cause: the Chinese bar is a living, breathing index of reform. Western interest in the Chinese bar, therefore, should be redoubled, as it may perhaps be the greatest bellwether for a future that will increasingly be dominated by Chinese interests.

The process of researching this book was exhilarating. It led us around the world, through prestigious universities and powerful boardrooms. It caused us to ponder the deepest questions of community, purpose, and prosperity. Through this project, we derived a sense of sobering awe at the monumental task of stabilizing and pacifying humanity. We sincerely hope that your experience in reading this book proves to be as rewarding as our experience in writing it.

Chapter 1

The Role of Lawyer

William Shakespeare immortalized his detestation of lawyers in *Henry VI* with the infamous quotation "First thing we do, let's kill all the lawyers." In the four hundred years since Shakespeare declared this agenda, resentment toward lawyers has proliferated and intensified. Given all of this resentment, it seems essential that before discussing Chinese lawyers, we should pause to reflect upon lawyers in general. If lawyers are so poorly perceived, why do they continue to thrive? Why are they so often reviled, and what benefits do they create that offset this revilement to justify their daily bread?

If one accepts the premise that organized government is a necessity of society, and one accepts the premise that courts of justice are a necessity of organized government, then the role of lawyers flows forth quite naturally.[1] If you must approach the court, either to seek relief for a wrong done to you or because someone is seeking relief from you, would you rather approach the court alone or with the help of someone whose entire life has been devoted to studying the behavior of the court? The answer is quite obvious: any rational person would prefer to approach the court with counsel. Of course, it would be even better to avoid situations that would require you to approach the court in the first place. Indeed, the legal profession is structured along these lines. Lawyers are divided into two primary categories: litigators and transactional lawyers. A simple way to understand the difference is to think of litigation as everything that happens when one goes to court, and transactional law as all of the precautions that one takes to avoid having to go to court. This includes negotiating and signing contracts, formalizing relationships through legally binding arrangements, and so on. Whether in court or in avoidance of court, the motivation to hire a lawyer comes from the desire for certainty. By hiring a lawyer, the client minimizes the uncertainty of whether and how the complaints of other citizens, the authority of the court, and the limitless power of the state will be brought to bear in the life of the individual.

In order to help clients most effectively, a lawyer must serve as her client's *faithful agent*. This means treating the client's interests and problems as though they were her own. This agency relationship is a crucial feature of the ethical ecology of lawyers. In order to safeguard the agency relationship, the lawyer must disentangle herself from and avoid all possible conflicts of interest. For this reason, lawyers are discouraged from engaging in business dealings with their clients. For the same reason, lawyers are ethically required to turn away a new client if representing that client could even possibly undermine the interests of an existing client. If the narrow interests of one additional client may be deemed a threat to the lawyer's ability to be a faithful agent, how much more so is that ability threatened by a broad organization with constellations of interests, such as the government or overactive professional societies? Lawyers need total independence so that they can choose and prosecute their arguments freely, respect confidentiality fully, and eliminate all conflicts of interests. To this extent, it is not enough that the individual lawyers be independent. The bar, representing all practitioners, must be an autonomous and independent service.

At first glance, lawyers seem to be at the heart of every dispute, from child-custody contests to neighbors' boundary suits, antitrust breakups, and even the Florida election battles. But not every dispute is fit for a lawyer to settle. Lawyers can only prevent and resolve *legally redressable* disputes. For example, a child has many interests—some of them are legally protected, others are not. Legally protected interests or rights are expressed in recognized legal sources, such as statutes, cases, and legal doctrine. Under the United States Uniform Marriage and Divorce Act, a child has the right to collect child support from his or her parents up until the age of maturity. To enforce this right, Congress created the Federal Parent Locator Service. The service permits any authorized individual to obtain and transmit information regarding an individual under an obligation to pay child support or to whom another owes a child-support obligation. Some states also permit courts to impose wage withholdings on obligors in noncompliance. Because child support is legally required for underage children, a lawyer can help a child or her guardian compel child support from a delinquent parent. On the other hand, children have an interest in living together with both parents until maturity, but this interest is not legally protected. Accordingly, no lawyer would waste her breath trying to convince a court to compel the parents to remain in the same domicile.

An essential part of a lawyer's job, therefore, is to help clients determine which of their interests are legally protected or can be argued as such. This is quite challenging, as laws are riddled with ambiguity and disputed interpretations. The idea of *the law* is a myth. *The law* is whatever the popular consensus understands the law to be, and that consensus is constantly in flux. For example, the legally protected right of civil marriage has undergone significant changes in the United States since the country's inception. In 1862 the United States Congress enacted the Morrill Anti-Bigamy Act, signed by Abraham Lincoln, which made bigamy a felony in the territories, punishable by a $500 fine or five years in prison. In 1882 the United States Congress passed the Edmunds Act, which allowed polygamists to be held indefinitely without a trial. In 1904 Mormons in Utah officially renounced polygamy, excommunicating anyone who participated in future polygamy. In 1967 the United States Supreme Court in *Loving v. Virginia* overturned antimiscegenation laws, or laws banning interracial couples from marrying. In 1996 President Bill Clinton signed the Defense of Marriage Act into law, defining marriage as a union between "a man and a woman." Under this Act, even if one state chooses to recognize a same-sex marriage, no other state is required to honor that marriage. This Act also prohibits the federal government from recognizing same-sex marriages. In 2004 and subsequently in 2008, Massachusetts and California recognized same-sex marriage. At the heart of each transformation is a dispute that featured not only two opposing clients but two opposing ideas: polygamy versus monogamy, monoracial marriages versus interracial marriages, and, ultimately, heterosexual marriages versus homosexual marriages. The lawyer arguing for each side does not submit to the contemporary consensus about the meaning of the law. Rather, she endeavors to forge a new consensus about the meaning of an existing law by emphasizing language that supports her position and minimizing language that weakens her position. By attempting to persuade the court that her client's interests are legally protectable, lawyers define and redefine the legal rights available to everyone.

Just as there are limits to what interests a lawyer may pursue, there are also limits to the extent to which she may pursue them. The most common perception among critics is that lawyers do one thing and one thing only: lie. Numerous lawyer jokes capitalize on this portrayal of lawyers, for example, "What do lawyers do when they die?" "Lie still." Here, the critics are not expressing disapproval of a horizontal resting position, they are expressing disapproval of false statements. In reality, the legal profession prohibits lawyers from making false statements. In the United States, the American Bar Association promotes legal ethics through the adoption of professional standards, most recently with the Model Code of Professional Responsibility, which was adopted by the House of Delegates on August 12, 1969, and subsequently by the vast majority of state and federal jurisdictions. Rule 4.1 of the Model Rules of Professional Conduct explicitly states,

> In the course of representing a client a lawyer shall not knowingly: (a) make a false statement of material fact or law to a third person; or (b) fail to disclose a material fact to a third person when disclosure is necessary to avoid assisting a criminal or fraudulent act by a client, unless disclosure is prohibited by Rule 1.6.

Similarly, rule 8.4(c) states, "It is professional misconduct for a lawyer to engage in conduct involving dishonesty, fraud, deceit or misrepresentation." Finally, per rule 3.4(b), "A lawyer shall not falsify evidence, counsel or assist a witness to testify falsely, or offer an inducement to a witness that is prohibited by law." If a lawyer is found to have violated any of the above rules, she could be subject to disciplinary action. Depending on the nature of misconduct, lawyers can be punished with disbarment, severe fines, or even jail time.

Ethical rules prohibit lawyers from making false statements, but they do not require that lawyers be honest. At first glance, this might strike the reader as a paradox. Aren't honesty and not making false statements the same thing? Where the law is concerned, they are not. Honesty entails full and unbiased disclosure of facts. A lawyer is not required to, and is in fact discouraged from disclosing facts that are unfavorable to her client. But short of making false statements, a lawyer is encouraged to be a zealous advocate whose disposition allows her to omit, edit, and tilt the truth as she sees fit to serve her client's best interests. After all, this is what it means to be a lawyer. Lawyers are professionals who are hired to be a mouthpiece for their client's legal interests.

Why doesn't the client represent her own interests? Why hire a mouthpiece? And if a mouthpiece must be hired, what makes a lawyer more suitable than anyone else? The answer is that the lawyer's training makes her better equipped to represent a client's interests than a layperson. While there are no "secret books" that only lawyers have access to, the law is so complex and voluminous that no one, not even the most knowledgeable lawyer, can understand it all. That is why most lawyers specialize, so that they can master a particular area of law in depth. Lawyers are also more familiar with the customs and procedures of the courtroom. Unrepresented parties often damage their own credibility or slow the court down as a result of their unfamiliarity. Another advantage lawyers possess over laypersons is familiarity with the norms of judicial interpretation of law. Even in the most transparent societies, legal texts alone do not indicate whether or how laws will be ultimately enforced and upheld. As an analogy, even though Illinois traffic laws unequivocally set the speed limit of the Stevenson Highway to be fifty-five miles per hour, a resident of Chicago may know that she can get away with driving three to seven miles per hour above the speed limit. She may know that radar guns of the local police force are not accurate enough to detect minute differences in speed. She may also know that the local government is simply not interested in chasing after small fines for driving marginally above the posted speed limit. Similarly, lawyers, through experience, are more familiar with where to find a law, what the law is, and how the law is likely to be enforced.

Having explained what lawyers do in their professional capacity, it is interesting to note the role that lawyers often play in government. Nearly all American presidents have been lawyers, Mahatma Gandhi was a lawyer, and David ben Gurion was a lawyer. Most American congressmen are lawyers, Felipe Calderón is a lawyer, and Nicolas Sarkozy is a lawyer. Even Vladimir Putin has a law degree! Lawyers seem to have a natural affinity for rising to the top echelon of governmental hierarchies in almost every country in the world. There are a few countries, however, where the top governmental posts are not occupied by lawyers. China is one such country. For example, Hu Jintao is a hydrological engineer, Wen Jiabao is a geological engineer, and Jiang Zemin is an electrical engineer. This suggests an interesting question: what is the difference between a government run by lawyers and one run by engineers? An engineer is someone who is skilled in creating. A lawyer is someone who is skilled in managing. The determination as to which skill set is needed most is a natural function of a country's developmental circumstances. When a country lacks adequate infrastructure, it promotes engineers to the top of the totem pole. Once infrastructure is built, the country promotes lawyers to the top of the totem pole. This pattern has been identified by Professor Alford, who advises us to "be mindful of the general 'generational' trajectory from soldiers to engineers to lawyers evident in Taiwan, Korea, and certain other jurisdictions."[2]

It seems very possible that China is about to enter the final stage of this generational trajectory. The first stage of generational trajectory was fulfilled by Mao Zedong, Zhou Enlai, and Deng Xiaoping, who were all revolutionaries. The second stage of generational trajectory was fulfilled by Jiang Zemin, Hu Jintao, and Wen Jiabao, who are all engineers. At the Seventeenth Party Congress of the Chinese Communist Party, two men were anointed as heirs-in-waiting for the top two posts in the government—president and premier. One of the two men, Xi Jinping, holds a PhD in law. No decision has been made as to which candidate will assume which office. Thus, there is a fifty-fifty chance that the next leader of the People's Republic of China will turn out to be a lawyer. Whether or not Mr. Xi ultimately assumes the top position, the fact that someone with legal training is even being considered for this post says a lot about the direction of the country. This trend is visible elsewhere as well. In 2008 *Caijing Magazine*, China's answer to *The Economist*, published a piece called "Faces to Watch." The piece asserted that there are twelve rising stars in the party. Two of them have degrees in engineering; four of them have PhDs in law.[3] Finally, the Shanghai municipal government regularly publishes a list of vacant positions and what sort of background is required for each position. According to the list published at the outset of 2008, nearly 10 percent of all vacancies require a degree in law.[4] For all of these reasons, it appears that China may very well be entering into the final stage of generational trajectory.

This chapter began with a question: *why does anyone need lawyers?* The question was answered, in part, by explaining the seemingly indispensable role that lawyers play in law and in government. After reading this chapter, Mr. Shakespeare might be disappointed to realize just how impractical it would be to kill all the lawyers.

Chapter 2

Cultural Background

Anyone who is engaged with China can tell you that Chinese lawyers represent an increasingly important element in business, government, and society. The goal of this book is to explain that growing importance and offer some insight into the future. In order to meet that goal, it may at first appear sufficient to expound the current status of Chinese lawyers. But the current status alone will mean nothing unless set in the proper context. Chinese lawyers are emerging today as the result of a hurricane clash of the most powerful forces of history, conflicting notions of righteousness, and willfully irreconcilable understandings of civilization. When set against this tumultuously charged background, it becomes apparent that the following account of Chinese lawyers is not merely the story of a rising group of professionals. It is at the very core of the story of the world's largest and oldest civilization entering into the modern age. It is the story of China standing upright after hundreds of years of slumber. It is no less than the story of the twenty-first century unfolding before our eyes.

Not a single individual, entity, or idea exists outside the sphere of impact generated by the events described in this narrative. As such, it is difficult to understand where the boundaries of this story begin and nearly impossible to determine where it will end. Our present task, situated somewhere in the middle, is to create enough distance between ourselves and the sequence of events in order to gain a perspective that will allow us to comprehend what is unfolding before us. The beginning of this process requires us to build a basic understanding of traditional China. This is the China that existed in isolation from the West. This is the China that for thousands of years constituted its own self-contained world. In fact, Chinese thinkers believed that China was the world, and the world was China. The name for China in Chinese is *Zhong Guo* (中国), meaning "Middle Kingdom."[1] From the traditional Chinese perspective, the only civilization in the world was the Chinese civilization, and the only thing that existed beyond China was borderland sparsely populated by barbarians. This view is somewhat understandable given that China's periphery was, indeed, populated rather sparsely by nomadic peoples lacking in the refinements of Chinese civilization. Direct contact with European or Semitic population centers which would have convinced the Chinese of the existence of other major civilizations simply did not exist.[2]

In the struggle to understand the world around them, the ancient predecessors of the Chinese people produced some of the world's earliest philosophy. This ancient philosophy was a highly sophisticated intellectual framework to answer the most significant questions that man has ever dared to ponder, namely, what is the origin of the universe and what is the nature of existence? The most masterful denizen of Chinese philosophy, Confucius, was born in 551 BCE, nearly one hundred years before the foundations of Western philosophy would be laid by Socrates.[3] Confucius canonized Chinese philosophy, but in doing so, he made it perfectly clear that the ideas he expounded were not his own, but rather, were the wisdom of the ancients.[4] The wisdom he promoted, therefore, carried not only the intellectual force of his own contribution, but the force of untold thousands of years of inherited refinement. With an intellectual accomplishment of this scale, it was no wonder that Chinese thinkers conceived of the non-Chinese world as barbarous.

The canon described above, collectively referred to as *the classics*, formed the backbone of traditional China, and its importance to traditional China cannot possibly be overstated.[5] It was believed that all wisdom, righteousness, propriety that could possibly exist was contained in the classics. The task of future generations was merely to tease it out through careful study and exegesis. Studying the classics and applying their lessons to contemporary problems was the noblest occupation to which one could aspire. All education, therefore, was geared toward exploration of the classics. The educational process began with large-scale memorization of the classics. After a student could recite entire tracts from memory, he would advance to the next stage of education, discussing the meaning of the classics. The final stage of education was writing original compositions in the style of the classics.

Much of what may be referred to as public policy was a matter of shrewdly applying the wisdom of the classics to the problems of the day. Interestingly, there was never any dogma about the classics. There was never a central authority to assert a singularly correct interpretation. The only correct interpretation was the one that proved unimpeachable in a given context, but that interpretation never acquired any sanctity or elevation. In a different context, it might be discarded. The interpretation and application of the classics, therefore, was a perpetually evolving endeavor that remained open to new voices, as long as they were educated voices. Moreover, it was believed that only a man who was learned in the classics could possess the moral and intellectual rectitude fit for public office. Government officials, therefore, were judged on their knowledge of the classics. Beginning in the Song Dynasty (960–1279 CE), aspirants to public office were subjected to the world's first civil-service examination, which was soon regularized to biannual schedule.[6] The basic exam was administered at the local level. The content of the exam tested the aspirant's knowledge of the classics in terms of memorization and in terms of the ability to form arguments that would apply classical wisdom to contemporary governmental and societal problems. If the aspirant did not pass, he was free to sit for the exam the next time around. If he did pass, he was invited to take a national-level exam. If he passed that exam, he was invited to take a third and final exam, which was administered in the capital by the emperor himself. Needless to say, this exam was exceedingly difficult. Anyone who was able to pass was immediately elevated and became an exalted creature, the object of envy of the entire kingdom. All those who passed the third exam were ranked according to performance. The high scorers were offered top positions in the central government, but all were guaranteed powerful positions as officials either in the central government or in the provinces.

The term for *official* in Chinese is *guan* (官), but it may as well be *demigod*, because the degree to which commoners would prostrate themselves before officials would suggest some level of sanctity.[7] In a certain sense, officials did possess a degree of sanctity. To the extent that the classics can be likened to a religion, officials of the highest rank who had passed the third level of examination had proven themselves accomplished religious scholars. It was only appropriate that some degree of sanctity reflected upon them. Furthermore, these officials were the handpicked deputies of the emperor, whose common appellation was *Son of Heaven*. Finally, officialdom was exalted for its significance in the realm of socioeconomic standing. The malevolence of nature made China a kingdom of unrelenting hardship, where basic survival required constant, backbreaking toil. Poverty, in the modern understanding of the term, was universal. The only escape from this poverty was elevation to the ranks of civil service, where official salary exceeded the cost of subsistence, even if not always by much. Business, land ownership, and any other conceivable source of wealth were ultimately synonymous with civil service because passing the civil-service exam required a profound education. Only a family already possessed of considerable wealth could afford the leisure necessary to educate a son to such an extent.[8] So, although the civil-service exam was in principle open to everyone, and it was hypothetically possible to go from rags to riches, it was very unlikely.[9] It was, however, possible for a family to dream of slowly accumulating enough resources over the course of several generations to educate one son sufficiently to pass the exam: "It was the common Chinese perception that individuals did not succeed; families with the support of their clans or lineages could."[10] Thus, common people viewed officials with absolute awe. They represented families that had labored through generations of struggle and achieved the dream of escaping from the cycle of poverty.

If the officials were demigods, surely the emperor was a god. There was no limit to the emperor's authority.[11] It was even said that "a minister has to perish if his ruler wants him to."[12] Although there was no limit to the emperor's authority, the emperor did not regularly exercise his unlimited authority. This is reflective of a general divergence between the principle and praxis of the imperial government.[13] In principle, China's form of government was absolute monarchy. In practice, it was locally autonomous democracy. In principle, the emperor wielded absolute power. In practice, the Chinese people enjoyed considerable freedom. Aside from performing certain ceremonial rites, the emperor was principally occupied with selecting officials to serve as his deputies in the provinces to collect taxes. In practice, this was the extent of the emperor's exercise of authority. The provincial officials played a similarly minimal role. In principle, each official presided over his province with the combined powers of executive, legislator, and judge. In practice, his activities were mostly confined to the collection of taxes. Certainly, if the provincial official were cruel or depraved, he could make himself a great burden on the people. And if he were benevolent and enlightened, he could lift the people up to great heights. But for the most part, he simply collected their taxes.

The real responsibilities of government, normally considered functions of the state, devolved down to the family.[14] The classics articulated a system of societal organization that was very family-centric and operated via a cascade of obligations. Each element of society was subject to certain obligations specific to his station, from the mightiest emperor to the smallest child. The emperor had obligations to his ministers, who in turn had obligations to magistrates, who in turn had obligations to provincial governors, who in turn had obligations to local leaders, who in turn had obligations to heads of households, who in turn had obligations specific to each member of the family. There was also a corresponding system of obligations directed upward from the individual child to the parent, to the leader of the clan, to the head of the village, and so on. Thus, Confucius wrote in the *Analects*, "Be filial, only be filial [towards your parents] and friendly towards your brothers, and you will be contributing to government."[15] The obligations were based on precepts of morality derived by the ancients from the heavenly order. The father of an individual family would run his household just as his father had done before him, according to the system of obligations articulated by the ancients and inherited through tradition. If a dispute arose within the family, it would be settled by the father according to the principles of the classics as best he understood them. If a dispute arose between families within the larger network of kinship, it would be settled by the elders of the clan according to the principles of the classics as best they understood them. It was very unlikely that a dispute would arise between two people who were not related through some network of kinship, because most villages contained only one or two clans. Thus, the informal system of arbitration through the family was adequate to resolve most disputes, and the majority of disputes were resolved in this forum. When, occasionally, a dispute arose between two people who were not related in any way, the dispute was adjudicated by the local magistrate. He would settle the dispute the same way that heads of families and clan elders settled disputes: according to the principles of the classics as best he understood them. Such officials were often referred to as *fumu guan* (父母官), or "parental officials."[16] Thus, the entire system of adjudication was perceived as intimate and filial.

Although the state's low level of involvement in governing the country might at first glance appear primitive, it was anything but. This arrangement afforded citizens maximum autonomy and assured minimum interference. This arrangement was the product of endless philosophical disquisition and hundreds of years of trial and error in the art of governance. This arrangement was the quintessential Jeffersonian dream. What made this dream a practical reality was the pervasiveness of the classical tradition: all interactions were predicated on universally shared expectations and values. In essence, cultural homogeneity ruled, while the state merely reigned.

According to Confucian thought, society would function mellifluously as long as everyone met their obligations. However, if at any level someone failed to meet his or her obligations, it would cause a disruption. If the disruption was not addressed, it would spread outward, generating discontent, unrest, and perhaps even rebellion against the individual who failed to meet the obligation. Under such circumstance, rebellion was legitimate. After all, anyone who did not meet his or her obligations was in defiance of the heavenly order and therefore did not deserve to retain his or her station. Rebellion would dislodge the offender from an undeserved position, to be replaced by someone with more reverence for the heavenly order. This applied to everyone, including the emperor. Such is the meaning of the phrase *mandate of heaven*.[17] As long as a dynasty reigned according to the will of heaven, it would continue to reign with the consent of heaven. But if it reigned in a way that offended the will of heaven, it would fall to rebellion and be replaced by a new dynasty. Thus, each emperor had an interest in being perceived as possessing the mandate of heaven. The best way to be perceived as such was to rule in accordance with the principles of morality outlined in the classics. For this reason, many emperors demonstrated rectitude, even if only for instrumental purposes. It was a system of checks and balances, albeit a clumsy one.[18]

This arrangement persisted for a full two thousand years, during which many dynasties rose and fell. As the vitality of a given dynasty faded and governance grew inept, a new dynasty would arise to supplant the old. Each new dynasty would make reference to the same classics in order to claim the mandate of heaven to justify its rule. The nomadic peoples on the borderlands collectively referred to as barbarians regularly attempted incursions in order to subjugate the Middle Kingdom. On two occasions, they succeeded. In order to reestablish order in the wake of their conquest, they immediately and opportunistically declared themselves the rightful heirs of the mandate of heaven. To prove their mandate, they set about demonstrating the qualities of leadership and the fulfillment of obligations specified by Confucius and the ancients. In other words, they began to act Chinese. The foreign invaders, originally intent on subjugating China, subtly became subjects of Chinese culture and were eventually drawn in by the gravity of Chinese civilization. This was the case with China's last dynasty, the Qing. The Qing Dynasty ruled China from 1644 till 1912. The dynasty was founded by an army of invading Manchus, ethnically and culturally distinct from Han Chinese. After conquering China, the Manchu ruling elite forced all Han Chinese men to wear long ponytails, called queues, to demonstrate loyalty to the foreign emperor.[19] This style involved a very long braid and shaving the pate. It is interesting to note that the queue eventually came to be accepted by Chinese men as a legitimate domestic fashion. So forceful was the gravity that Chinese civilization exerted on the rest of the world that both King George III of England as well as George Washington adopted a variant of the queue, which came to be regarded in the West as something of Oriental high fashion, or chinoiserie.[20]

Gradually but certainly, the center of Manchu civilization shifted into China proper and was eventually consumed by the sheer gravity of Chinese civilization. In this light, the establishment of two foreign dynasties

FIGURE 1. King George III and George Washington.

Source. Adapted from Google Images.

was never perceived to invalidate the basic premise of traditional Chinese political philosophy, but was seen, rather, as a hearty confirmation thereof. The fact that foreigners wanted to enter China and seek positions of authority merely served to confirm the notion that China was the center of the world. And the fact that foreigners embraced the classics served to confirm the notion that the classics contained universal truths equally applicable to the whole of mankind and that there really was a *mandate of heaven* which was predicated upon the embrace of those truths. The two foreign dynasties, then, were seen as endorsements of Chinese civilization rather than any sort of abrogation.

Throughout the two-thousand-year history of imperial China, there was a constant cycle of old dynasties decaying and new dynasties supplanting them, usually through hostile means. Occasionally, the new dynasty would emerge from the periphery of Chinese civilization. When that dynasty began to decay, it would be replaced by a new dynasty of thoroughly domestic origin. Each time, the new dynasty would claim the mandate of heaven by making reference to the classics. This cycle can be likened to the motion of a great pendulum. The chain which suspends the pendulum represents the Chinese people themselves, locked arm to arm across space and time, while the weight at the bottom of the pendulum which provides it with momentum is representative of the classics. The pendulum swings back and forth, each time swinging a bit too far in one direction, but each time returning to the center. The pendulum was in motion for two thousand years, constantly dancing around equilibrium. The frequent nudge of barbarous tribes attempting invasion from China's periphery might create an unanticipated impetus upon the pendulum, but the gravity of the classics and the tenacity of the people kept the pendulum moving in a circumscribed manner. It seemed perfectly reasonable to believe that this system would continue in perpetuity, that this was all of human existence. The gravity of the classics and the tenacity of the people kept this remarkable system in motion for two thousand years, until the inconceivable occurred: a moving body with even greater momentum collided with the pendulum's path of motion, permanently derailing it, tearing its weight and tether asunder.

This new moving body of greater momentum was many things. It was rival canons with their own notions of righteousness. It was unprecedented advancement in science and technology. It was hundreds of years of fierce interstate competition. It was Western civilization.

China was never truly isolated from the West. Historical records show that concern regarding a one-way stream of commerce between China and the West dates as far back as the beginning of the Roman Empire. From 31 BCE to 192 CE, Rome sustained a trade deficit with China of nearly $9 billion.[21] But this commerce was not transacted directly between East and West; rather, it took place via an enormous and unorganized network of intermediaries along the Silk Road.[22] These intermediaries, nomadic merchants, would emerge from Central Asia to purchase large quantities of Chinese goods such as porcelain and silk. Regarded as barbarians, they had to pay tribute for the privilege of engaging in trade with the Middle Kingdom.[23] The practice of demanding tribute reinforced the notion that Chinese civilization was the only civilization by demonstrating that engagement with the Middle Kingdom was a universally sought-after privilege. When the merchants had acquired enough goods, they would journey to the West, disappearing beyond the horizon of Chinese periphery. The goods would change hands many times along the road to Rome, but none of this was visible from the Chinese perspective. From the Chinese perspective, the only visible features were nomads, barbarians, and tribute.

This perspective of the world outside of China was enhanced by occasional incursions by people who were quite aptly described by the term *barbarians*. They would mount unorganized and flimsy campaigns in an attempt to invade and plunder the Middle Kingdom. The imperial army would be summoned to put down these incursions, which were rarely challenging. This served to reinforce the notion that the world outside of China was populated by barbarians who wanted desperately to partake in Chinese civilization.

This perspective was undisturbed for over a thousand years. Around the sixteenth century, a new variety of foreigner arrived in the Middle Kingdom. Missionaries were drawn to China by the lure of saving hundreds of millions of souls, none of whom were aware of a need of being saved.[24] Attempts at proselytizing were generally unsuccessful. One missionary quipped, "The Chinese are so self-opinionated that they cannot be made to believe that the day will ever come when they will learn anything from foreigners which is not already set down in their own books."[25] His comment reflects indignation at the notion that Chinese civilization was the universal civilization, conceiving of no value or role for other cultures. In a humorously comparable demonstration of cultural absolutism, the pope

> sent papal legates to the court of the Kangxi Emperor about 1700 to forbid as idolatrous…Chinese family-centered rituals. The emperor, whose authority in matters of Chinese politics and culture recognized no bounds, found the pope's envoys, French clerics of highest standing, to be illiterate (in the relevant language) and ignorant, so sent them packing.[26]

The point is that until the last years of the eighteenth century, all of China's contacts with the outside world were confined to individuals or small cohorts of individuals, often legitimately barbarian. Those individuals who were not barbarians were nonetheless regarded as barbarians because, from the Chinese perspective, the great civilizations with whom they intermediated were out of view, their achievements unperceivable. They were understood to be *wai yi* (外夷), or "outer barbarians"—just like the uncivilized nomads of Mongolia and Central Asia, except originating from further away.[27] It was not until the late eighteenth century that the achievements of Western civilization became directly visible to a Chinese audience.

Before the dawn of the Industrial Revolution, China accounted for a dominant share of global output, substantially explained by the fact that China accounted for a dominant share of global population. The Industrial Revolution represented a new age in which a man's product was not confined to the sum of his labor but was rather a multiple of his labor, the magnitude of which depended on the productivity of the technology he could devise. The old rules were out. Under the new rules, a larger population did not guarantee a larger or better product. China's attitude

Figure 2. Italian Jesuit Matteo Ricci preaching in Beijing, circa 1600.

Source. Kircher (1667).

toward foreigners was formed under the old rules: as long as the barbarians were willing to pay tribute and conduct themselves with civility, they would be allowed to purchase Chinese goods. Consideration was never given to purchasing goods from foreigners because prior to the Industrial Revolution, China possessed everything the foreigners possessed and then some. But by the end of the eighteenth century, it was no longer the case that the West had nothing to offer.

At this time in China, there was no ministry of foreign affairs. Foreign affairs, in the sense that we understand the concept, did not exist.[28] What would foreign affairs mean to a society that considered itself the only civilization in the world? What would be the purpose of a ministry of foreign affairs? Any barbarians that entered into the civilized realm would be dealt with in a fashion befitting the circumstances, but their existence was never thought to necessitate any agency or organized response.

The West sought to establish peaceful trading relations with China. In pursuit of this goal, King George III of England sent an ambassadorial mission to the court of the Qianlong emperor in 1793, at which time the emperor was eighty-two years old. Respectful of Chinese protocol, the mission offered to the emperor a tribute of lavish gifts. The mission requested rights to sell British manufactured goods at Chinese ports. The notion of buying goods from barbarians struck the emperor as peculiar.

> The old emperor treated the British demands as if they came from a small tribe in Inner Asia...yet he undoubtedly could see that Great Britain presented him with an entirely different scale of challenge. He apparently did not have the will or the intellectual energy at that late moment in his life to do more than fall back on traditional attitudes and formalities in the hopes of dismissing an intractable problem.[29]

The emperor's famous rejection to King George read, "We possess all things. I set no value on objects strange or ingenious, and have no use for your country's manufactures."[30]

To the British crown, the concept of giving up a potential commercial advantage simply because of initial resistance was absolutely inconceivable. British policy toward China quickly acquired an aggressive character, resolving to crack open the Chinese market by force if necessary. In the deadlocked competition of mercantilist imperialism, wherever Britain sought a commercial opportunity, her continental rivals were sure to follow. Soon, the whole of Europe was engaged with China like a pearl diver with an oyster, intent on smashing it open by whatever means necessary to access to the precious treasure within.

But China's leaders did not see the storm gathering on the horizon. As of 1800, China's leaders remained fully confident in their tradition. The ensuing hundred years would disabuse them of many of the notions of a Sinocentric world order, including the divinity of the emperor and the completeness and universality of classical wisdom.

After failing to establish trading relations, Britain endeavored to balance the flow of trade by smuggling opium into China and encouraging a national addiction. Opium was outlawed in China, but where demand exists for a good, no amount of government proscription will prevent it from being supplied. Britain was in strong supply of opium from the poppy fields of its colonial possession in nearby South Asia. Britain's endeavor proved fabulously successful. By the 1820s, China imported nearly one thousand tons of opium per year. When the emperor's appointed drug czar, Lin Zexu, made a moralistic plea to the British crown that it should not encourage in China the consumption of a substance which was illegal in Britain, his words fell on deaf ears.[31] When he attempted to disrupt the inflow of opium, Britain responded with bellicose hostility. In June of 1840, the HSS *Nemesis* razed the port city of Guangdong and then sailed up the Yangtze River, dispensing mortar rounds and crippling the imperial infrastructure.[32] The Treaty of Nanjing, signed in 1843, would prove to be a temporary peace. Hostilities of this nature would erupt over and over again throughout the course of the nineteenth century.[33] China's emperors were forced to concede every time owing to the West's overwhelming military superiority. The Western powers treated each concession as a foothold for further exactions. More port cities were wrenched opened to foreign trade. With each additional port came new products, and with each new product came more demands about the legal-governmental environment in which trade would be prosecuted. As these demands proliferated, they intruded abruptly into the sovereign space of the emperors. Shanghai was divided up into spheres of influence. There was a British sphere, a French sphere, an American sphere, and so on. Hong Kong was ceded to Britain, Macau was ceded to Portugal, and Qingdao was ceded to Germany. It became startlingly clear that a major change in governance was occurring. This event, unique in Chinese history, was distinguished by the fact that the foreigners did not make a claim on the mandate of heaven. They made no pretense about meeting traditional expectations of imperial obligations. In short, they did not even pay salutary lip service to the classics. The fact that the outer barbarians were able with such ease to put down the forces of the emperor, who espoused classical virtue, for the first time called into question the wisdom of the ancients and, indeed, the entire cosmological framework on which the imperial order was built.

It is against this backdrop that lawyers were introduced to Chinese civilization. As trade between China and the rest of the world increased, foreign merchants insisted that the Beijing government provide them with the same business-legal formalities to which they were accustomed.[34] They demanded contracts to codify terms of delivery and payment, legal institutions to offer redress for broken contracts, and legal professionals who could navigate these institutions and contracts on their behalf.

These demands did not sit well with the emperors. Any time foreigners challenged the conventions of their rule, let alone its legitimacy, the emperors considered it not only a threat to their power but also an impeachment of their entire worldview. Needless to say, they did not respond well to demands from European merchants. But beyond the indignation at the simple fact that demands were being made of them, the emperors took offense at the nature of what was being demanded, which was fundamentally at odds with tradition. Compared to the intimacy of family-centered adjudication based on the principles of the classics, a formal legal system of adjudicating disputes seemed cold and inert. Moreover, it seemed to trivialize the divine rule of the emperor. If someone could be proven right without referencing the forces of history and society that had installed the emperor on his seat of power, then this would indicate that right existed outside of the emperor, a contradiction of the basic premise of the imperial system.

As such, the imperial establishment resisted embracing legal reforms. One nineteenth-century emperor issued an edict decrying the growing ranks of *litigation tricksters*: "These rascally fellows entrap people for the sake of profit…At their bidding plaintiffs are induced to bring up stupid nonsense in their accusations."[35] The edict stipulated that anyone who made a living by preparing legal petitions for others would be severely punished. But, ultimately, where market demand for a service exists, no amount of government proscription will prevent the service from being provided. One of the many concessions that the foreign powers exacted was the codification of imperial law, which hitherto had been a collection of ad hoc decrees lacking any semblance of organization. In 1910 the Criminal and Civil Code of the Great Qing was published. This document was the first instance of the word *lawyer* appearing in print.[36] A brief digression into the etymology of the Chinese term for *lawyer* will provide some insight into the role of lawyers in Chinese society, both in traditional and modern times.

The Chinese word that is commonly translated into English as "law" is *falü* (法律). This is composed of two characters, *fa* (法) and *lü* (律). Depending on context, the word *fa* means method, principle, or flow. Although each of these concepts may seem unrelated, the complex of meaning is made sensible by an explanation of the way the character is drawn. The left half of the character means "water," and the right half of the character is the verb "to go." The meaning we draw from this is that there is a principle or method associated with the flow of water. No matter where you place water, it always flows to equilibrium, levels off, and seeks to occupy the lowest space possible. Ancient scholars explained that this concept is relevant in law.[37] The law levels society, according to principle. Later in Chinese history, the word *fa* acquired a Buddhist meaning. It came to be the Chinese term for *dharma*, essentially, "the inexorable truth." The word *lü* means "regulated." The earliest uses of the word *lü* were in reference to tuned musical instruments. Later on,

Cultural Background   31

the word came to mean "regulations," in the legal sense. The term *falü* is conventionally translated as "law." Although there is nothing wrong with this translation, we should remain aware at some level that the term is wrapped in layers of additional meaning: principle, leveling, truth, and regulation.

The word *lawyer* is translated as *lüshi* (律师). The term *lüshi* was used as early as the Tang Dynasty in nonlegal capacities related to Buddhism and Taoism. The legal sense of the term first came into use at some point during the Qing (1644–1911), China's last dynasty. The meaning of the first character, *lü*, has already been explained. The second character, *shi*, means "specialist." Thus, the combination can be taken to mean a regulation specialist. It is interesting to note that the lofty ideals of principle, leveling, and truth conveyed by *fa* are not explicitly present in the term for lawyer, *lüshi*. The only meaning explicitly conveyed by *lüshi* is "regulation specialist." It could be argued that *lüshi* is a contraction for *falüshi*, and therefore, the other shades of meaning are implied. However, it could also be said that the contraction *fashi* was not adopted into regular speech; the contraction *lüshi* was. So, at one level or another, the Chinese word for *lawyer* prioritizes regulation over principle, leveling, and truth. From this perspective, it is evident that, in the most fundamental sense, Chinese civilization conceived of a narrow role for lawyers. But even this narrow role was a tight squeeze.

Lawyers were perceived as charlatans who were out to ensnare people in a web of litigation in order to trick them out of their money. Accordingly, in popular discourse, lawyers were generally referred to as *songgun* (讼棍), or "litigation tricksters."[38] Some readers may react to this perception with sympathy, echoing the preponderance of lawyer jokes in the West. However, there is a fundamental difference. Lawyer-bashing in the West is based on common sensations of dilemma that accompany the experience of being a party to litigation. However, underneath all of the jokes, there is awareness that lawyers provide society with beneficial services, such as defense of civil liberties, organization of government, and other public goods. In China during the latter years of the Qing Dynasty, lawyers were not perceived as providers of these public goods because this was not their province. Legitimacy, authority, and the forces that organize society flowed forth from the classics. Lawyers were not perceived to be defenders of civil liberties because no such concept existed in the Chinese polity. Lawyers were perceived as contributing nothing beneficial to society because their entire sphere of activity was confined to litigation, often on behalf of foreign interests. In the absence of the positive perceptions that accompany the provision of public goods, there was nothing to mitigate the negative perceptions that accompany litigation. As a result, attitudes toward lawyers were purely malignant. Lawyers were perceived as a virulent plague imposed by the West in order to weaken China through internal decay.

The foreign powers persisted in demanding further legal reforms.[39] Whenever Beijing would resist undertaking legal reforms, representatives of the Western powers would threaten exaction and invasion. Ultimately, Beijing would acquiesce to each demand. Thus, legal culture, institutions, and professionals were introduced to China under conditions of duress. This would influence Chinese popular attitudes toward lawyers for the next hundred years.

Each time the emperor would acquiesce to foreigners' demands, legal or otherwise, it diminished the emperor's bona fides in the eyes of the people, and they gradually began to question the rationality of the imperial system. How could the emperor be so utterly impotent vis-à-vis the barbarians? How did they manage to overpower him if they did not possess, and were not interested in possessing, the mandate of heaven? There arose a crisis of faith in the legitimacy of the emperor, the classics, and tradition. Young men, in particular, were affected by the results of this confrontation. Psychologists say that when a young man sees his father's masculinity diminished, it provokes a mixed reaction of shame and anger. When the young men of China saw their national father repeatedly emasculated, a high-pressured atmosphere of shame and anger enveloped Chinese cities. Young men began to lash out at the established order and all things traditional. In a gesture of great symbolism, many young men even cut off their queues. In the spring of 1911 in Changsha, the capital city of Hunan Province, a young man named

Mao Zedong cut off his queue. Exhibiting a pattern of behavior that would foreshadow later events, he also pinned down all of his friends and forcibly cut off their queues as well.[40]

Anxiety and discontent grew day by day until it found expression in the Wuchang Uprising on October 10, 1911.[41] By the end of the year, full-scale revolution was under way, and Emperor Puyi abdicated the throne on February 12, 1912, ending the last imperial dynasty in China.

Two prominent trends marked the period of time following the downfall of the Qing Dynasty. The first trend was a castigation of the classics. People began to refer to Confucius as an apologist for feudalism who was incompatible with the modern world. In language typical of the day, one Chinese editorialist wrote,

> It is said in chapter thirty of the Book of Rites that "while parents are living, the son dares not regard his person or property as his own." This is absolutely not the way to personal independence…In all modern constitutional states, whether monarchies or republics, there are political parties. Those who engage in party activities all express their spirit of independent conviction. They go their own way and need not agree with their fathers or husbands. When people are bound by the Confucian teachings of filial piety and obedience to the point of the son not deviating from the father's way even three years after his death and the woman obeying not only her father and her husband but also her son, how can they form their own political party and make their own choice? The movement of women's participation in politics is also an aspect of women's life in modern civilization. When they are bound by the Confucian teaching that "to be a woman means to submit," that "the wife's words should not travel beyond her own apartment," and that "a woman does not discuss affairs outside the home," would it not be unusual if they participated in politics?[42]

The second trend was a power vacuum in the political arena. After the downfall of the Qing, competing political parties and warlords vied for supremacy for most of the next forty years. Gradually, the Nationalist Party (KMT) consolidated control over China from the capital they established in Nanjing in 1925. The KMT was much more hospitable to the practice of law than its imperial predecessor.[43] Senior leaders in Nanjing, perceiving legality as the organizational bedrock that made Western governments so strong, sought to encourage the study and practice of law. The manner in which the KMT interacted with the outside world concerning reform and the building of legal culture was diametrically opposed to the manner of its predecessor. Whereas Western powers had to force legal reform upon the Qing, the KMT sent emissaries abroad to study foreign legal systems. The legal profession was aided by the character of Nationalist law. The precision and clarity of the laws promulgated by the KMT were without precedent in Chinese history. All else being equal, a right that is defined precisely is easier to defend than a right that is defined vaguely. A legal process that is defined clearly is easier to undertake than a legal process that is defined vaguely. As a result, lawyers flourished under the Nationalists. In 1912 there were about three thousand lawyers nationally.[44] By 1935, there were over ten thousand lawyers nationally.[45]

These promising inroads toward legal development were severely frustrated by Japan's attempt to conquer and colonize China. Although the Nationalists had achieved supremacy, the KMT's chief adversary was never completely eliminated. This adversary was the Communist Party, and the rivalry between the two groups was absolutely vitriolic. When Japanese aggression heated up, however, defense against foreign aggression occupied a higher place on the hierarchy of priorities than prevailing in internal political disputes. At the end of December 1936, the Communists, led by Mao Zedong, gathered at Xi'an to force a truce upon the Nationalists, who were led by Jiang Jieshi. The treaty stipulated that the two parties would form a common front, fighting together to repel the Japanese and free China from foreign influence once and for all. In reality, neither Mao nor Jiang had any intention of honoring the spirit of the treaty. They both looked at this as an opportunity to pit one enemy against another. They both intended to turn on one another the moment that it became expedient to do so. Of course, when there is a shared awareness that both sides are gunning to defect, a race will inevitably develop to be the first to defect. As a result, both sides worked to undermine each other even before the Japanese incursion was neutralized. The Communist Party ultimately triumphed over the Nationalist Party in 1949, and Mao Zedong ascended to the pinnacle of the Forbidden City. From this historical seat of imperial power, he proclaimed the birth of the People's Republic of China (PRC). The next several years were spent consolidating the absolute political power of the Communist Party.

One of the chief functions of lawyers is the management of private property rights. Marxism denies the validity of private property rights. In Marxist philosophy, law is an instrument of class domination, a way to preserve the riches of the rich and keep shackles on the poor. Almost immediately after the establishment of the PRC, Mao abolished the legal profession and system of legal education that had existed under the Nationalists, as well as the entire body of laws that had governed China until that point.[46] In its place, he established a Ministry of Justice (MOJ) to rubber-stamp the legality of government decisions.

Whenever a coup successfully overturns a government, the lawyers are almost invariably the first to go. Lawyers earn their daily bread through their knowledge of the law. The law is given by the government. Therefore, as a group, lawyers have an incentive to preserve the government that promulgated the law under which they were trained. Mao's suspicion of the Nationalist lawyers, therefore, was not entirely unreasonable. However, the notion that a modern government could be run without any lawyers would not pan out.

By 1954, it was clear that China needed lawyers. With all of the domestic lawyers purged and no relations with the West, China turned north to the Soviet Union for guidance. In 1955 an experimental system of lawyers based on the Soviet *advokatura* system was established in the large cities.[47] These advocates, employees of the state, were trained in socialist legal principles. Their function was to extend the reach of the state by regulating basic matters such as marriage. They were not expected to, nor were they allowed to, involve themselves in matters of political or economic import.

In 1956 the Hundred Flowers Campaign was launched. Chairman Mao famously declared, "Let one hundred flowers bloom," meaning, let one hundred schools of thought emerge. In this apparent call for a marketplace of ideas, the government invited all intellectuals to put forth proposals for how the system of governance could be improved. The altruistic individuals who thought that their insight was genuinely invited would become victims of a government trap to identify and eliminate reactionaries. Unfortunately, many lawyers participated in the Hundred Flowers Campaign. As a result of this involvement, the lawyers were purged again in 1957. By 1959, the Ministry of Justice was abolished. Finally, when the Cultural Revolution began in 1966, the remaining lawyers were completely eradicated.[48]

The next ten years were utter anarchy. Students beating teachers, officials crawling through the streets wearing dunce caps, grandparents making public apologies to their grandchildren for clinging to the old ways as generations of family heirlooms burned bright in the streets—these were all common sights during the Cultural Revolution. This period of time, almost unique in modern history, is a valuable illustration of the role of law. Such anarchy normally emerges only in the context of war. The absence of war during the Cultural Revolution demonstrates that chaos is not caused by the presence of war but rather by the absence of law. The exact motivation behind the Cultural Revolution remains unclear to this day. Was it about "throw[ing] off the bonds of thousands of years of old thinking and old customs," as official rhetoric insisted?[49] Or was it about eliminating dissent within the Party and consolidating control over the people? Or was it about nothing, merely a product of Mao's dementia? The great likelihood is that it was a combination of all three.

The depravity persisted until Chairman Mao died in September of 1976. Ten years of turmoil came to a close as the Cultural Revolution finally ended. With Mao's exit, a new power vacuum emerged. Many of the government leaders who vied for power after 1976 had been victims of the arbitrary brutality of the Cultural Revolution, including Deng Xiaoping.[50] As a result, when Deng achieved supremacy in 1978, one of his chief priorities was to reestablish order. The Chinese people also craved order. Without a doubt, the willingness that the Chinese citizenry has demonstrated repeatedly in the last thirty years to subordinate civil liberties to order is a direct result of the experience of the Cultural Revolution.

In 1978, under the direction of Deng, the government adopted the Opening Up and Reform Policy. In 1979 Deng took initial steps toward reinventing the legal system. That year, the system of lawyers was revived and legal education resumed.[51] The Beijing Lawyers Association and the Ministry of Justice were rededicated. The Ministry of Justice was tasked with creating a functioning judiciary. Given that the most prominent and talented legal thinkers had all been eliminated in the campaigns of the last thirty years, it was impossible to find enough jurists to breathe life into the *corpus juris*. The Ministry of Justice's solution to the dearth of qualified judges was to synthesize them from army officers; the government simply transferred retired and retiring officers from the ranks of the military to the benches of the courtroom.[52] Military officers, like judges, are responsible for making consequential decisions. Additionally, the patriotism and loyalty of military officers is unyielding. As such, military officers should make effective judges…or so the thinking went. Absent in this logic was an appreciation for the judicial mindset that comes about only as a result of years of thinking about legal problems.

The Ministry of Justice also failed to appreciate the economics of corruption. A public official will choose to engage in corruption only if doing so yields more benefits than costs. On the one hand, participating in corruption can generate great benefits, usually in money or influence. On the other hand, participating in corruption can result in great costs. Society imposes sanctions, generally with uncertain probability, on public officials who engage in corruption. Once they get caught, public officials will most certainly lose, among other valuables, their title and reputation. In a merit-based system, title and reputation require time and energy to cultivate. For example, in order to become a judge in the United States, one must first become an attorney by obtaining a degree of Juris Doctor (JD), passing a state's bar examination, and gaining experience practicing law. Judges must first become lawyers because it is assumed that lawyers will understand better than nonlawyers how to apply and interpret laws in a way that best resolves individual and societal problems. After becoming a lawyer, the next step is to apply for a judgeship when there is an opening in a court of preference. The procedure for this will vary, depending on the jurisdiction and type of court. Due to the competitive nature of the field, the candidate will then need political support to be appointed or elected. Initially, it is also necessary to impress judicial-nominating commission members, especially for state judgeships. Once appointed or elected, new judges are required to undergo orientation and training. After that, judges must attend continuing education courses and seminars throughout their careers. Judges in the United States are normally appointed for long periods of time. Most federal judges, except for some, like bankruptcy (fourteen years) and federal claims court (fifteen years), are appointed for life. Because it takes so much time and effort to build a judicial career in the United States, seasoned judges are less willing to gamble their hard-earned reputation and judgeship away in a game of corruption.

Such was not the case in China. Retired and retiring military officers who threw on judges' robes did not have to invest anything in a legal education or developing a reputation for legal excellence. To them, the value of a career that was practically handed to them paled in comparison to the rewards that could be reaped from corruption. Additionally, because these military officers became judges in midcareer or later, the number of years that they would be expected to work as judges was relatively small. As a result, the value to them of their judicial reputation was very small, and the minimum payoff that would be needed to make it economically efficient for them to undertake corruption was very small.

In order to meet the demand for prosecutors, the government transferred civil servants from other departments into the prosecutor's office. In Chinese, the judges, prosecutors, police, and all other actors on the governmental side of prosecution are collectively referred to as *gongjianfa* (公检法). The original generation of *gongjianfa*, almost entirely drawn from other organs of the government and military, entered upon their duties without any legal education or experience.

In 1980 the Beijing Bureau of Justice was revived and the National People's Congress (NPC) passed the Provisional Regulations on Lawyers, which officially defined lawyers as "state legal workers."[53] A contemporary memorial stated that

> Chinese lawyers are state legal workers. They are not professionals in the Western sense. They shoulder highly political and professional tasks and obligations…In other words, politically, lawyers should be patriots first and foremost, and at the same time, they are revolutionaries who firmly adhere to the socialist road. By satisfying these two basic political requirements, lawyers working within socialist laws serve the fundamental interests of the state and the people by performing their services and guaranteeing the proper functioning of the socialist legal system.[54]

Initially, most of the work of the new generation of lawyers was in criminal defense.[55] Given that judges and prosecutors are state employees, it may strike the reader as odd for criminal defense to also be supplied exclusively by state employees. If the prosecutor, judge, and defender are all paid by the state, wouldn't this stack the deck against the defendant? However, one must remember the tenuous context that surrounded the revival of the legal profession. Lawyers were systematically purged in 1949 and 1957 and then completely eradicated in 1966. When the profession was officially revived in 1979, students were not exactly eager to become lawyers. It stood to reason that the "official revival" might have been another trap. Any lawyers that may have survived the tribulations of the last twenty years were painfully aware of the potential consequences of returning to the profession. Unfortunately, it was precisely these individuals that the government expected to fill China's needs for legal counsel. In this context, how could they be expected to enter a courtroom and argue against a judge, prosecutor, or policeman? This amounted to arguing against the state! As a result, the decision to declare lawyers as "state legal workers" can be understood as a political compromise, a guarantee of some level of protection for lawyers in exchange for their willingness to come forward and meet the government's urgent need for legal services.[56]

Deng's Opening Up and Reform Policy created the urgent demand.[57] The logic of the Opening Up and Reform Policy was that if China opened up, investment would pour in from all around the world. This was premised on the fact that China, at the time, had the cheapest cost of labor anywhere in the world and ample natural resources. But, curiously, foreign investment did not immediately follow China's opening. "A prominent legal scholar in China who has written extensively on Chinese lawyers and who served on the drafting team of the 1996 Lawyers Law argues explicitly that laws and lawyers were developed in the early years of China's reform period to create the institutional appearance of a rational legal system necessary to attract foreign investment:

> In the beginning, after the Eleventh Party Congress [in 1979], China built special economic zones. These special economic zones were built to attract investment from foreign enterprises and enterprises outside the boundaries of mainland China, including foreign investment from enterprises in Hong Kong and Taiwan. However, in the early 1980s many people came to look, but very few actually invested. The state thought it was very strange because in China at the time the price of labor was the cheapest in the world and there were special tax discounts—at the time the first three years were tax-free. Later there were even more tax breaks; there were wonderful discounts at the time. And a lot of money could be saved on raw materials. At the time the thinking of the central government was that if they just opened the nation's gates, foreign enterprises would come flooding in. Only later did they realize that this was not the case. So they conducted some investigations to find out why it wasn't the case. I recall that at the time some officials from the China Merchants Shekou Industrial Zone in Shenzhen [the first "open industrial zone" in China] told the central government that it was very strange. Many managers and bosses of foreign enterprises came to look around. They'd look at the investment environment and ask about investment policies. There were never any problems about this. But then they asked, does China have law? Are there any lawyers? At the time in Shenzhen, many of the people working in the Merchants Bureau had no idea if China had any lawyers. But they could say that China had law. They said we have a *Constitution*, a *Marriage*

Law, a *Criminal Law*, a *Criminal Procedure Law*. At the time we really did have these laws. The *Criminal Law* and *Criminal Procedure Law* were promulgated in 1979. We've had the *Marriage Law* since 1954. And we've always had the *Constitution*. We say we have law, but you say we don't: there's no law for economic matters, no *Company Law*, no *Enterprise Law*, and no *Securities Law*. With respect to lawyers, the people in the Merchants Bureau inquired and learned that, yes, there are lawyers. At the time, in 1980, or actually in 1979, Deng Xiaoping said we should revive lawyers. So in 1980 there were lawyers. So you say there are lawyers. How come I don't see any on the street? Why are there no signs for law firms? Well, our lawyers belong to the Bureau of Justice. At the time we didn't call them law firms; they were called legal advisory offices and were departments within the Bureau of Justice. We said this is where our lawyers work. Later people studied China's lawyers and concluded that this system was unacceptable. Why? These lawyers of yours are state legal workers, right? These lawyers are on the state payroll. So, when I run into a legal dispute and need to file a court petition, you're all part of the state, your companies are all state-owned companies, your lawyers are state legal workers. So who will represent our foreign interests? Who will speak on our behalf? So foreigners didn't dare invest. Only then did China realize that if they want to attract foreign investment, they need to consider more than whether or not money can be made.[58]

This epiphany prompted a period of privatization and reform that lasted from the early 1980s until 2002. In 1980 all Chinese lawyers worked for the state, as stipulated by the Provisional Regulations on Lawyers. The organizational units in which lawyers worked were originally called *Legal Advisory Offices*.[59] In 1984 the name *Legal Advisory Office* was officially replaced with *law firm*.[60] Nonetheless, these law firms were still units of the state. Each firm would receive money from the government in accordance with the number of slots they occupied in the state personnel allocation system.[61] In return, the fees generated by lawyers were given to the government. In 1986 the All China Lawyers Association (ACLA) was created.[62] Although there are several prominent differences, the ACLA is the Chinese analogue to the American Bar

Association (ABA). Also in 1986, the first national lawyers' examination was administered by the Ministry of Justice.[63]

In 1988 the legal field was substantially liberalized by the introduction of the cooperative law firm model.[64] Cooperative law firms were still state-owned, but they were not a part of the state personnel allocation system.[65] Instead, they were self-accounting and had the discretion to hire and fire employees at will. This was the opening foray in the privatization of the legal industry. The imperative of privatization was based on two observations. The first observation was that the limited capacity of China's lawyers to provide legal services would cripple economic growth unless the bar was substantially expanded. This prompted the government to establish an official goal of licensing 150,000 lawyers by the turn of the century.[66] The second observation was that if lawyers were to remain on the state payroll, then expanding the bar to 150,000 would be at odds with the broader trends of downsizing the civil service and withdrawing the government from the economy, and would perhaps be financially unsustainable. These two observations made privatization of the bar a necessity.

Privatization took a great leap forward in 1992 with the introduction of the partnership law firm model. Unlike cooperative firms, partnership firms are completely privately owned and operated.[67] The only significant government regulation of partnership law firms is that they are required to employ at least three lawyers. The attractiveness of this loose regulatory supervision helps explain why the partnership model quickly supplanted the cooperative model and state-owned model as the most popular structure for organizing a law firm. It also helps to explain why the legal profession would go on to become one of the fastest-growing career paths for young Chinese. "Three full-time lawyers can open a law firm, but three journalists cannot open a news agency. This vast space for development is undoubtedly extremely attractive to young people"[68] considering what career options to pursue.

As the question of how legal groups would be organized was answered by the privatization of the industry, the question of who a lawyer was came to the fore. According to the 1980 Provisional Regulations on

Lawyers, an individual did not have to pass any sort of test to qualify for admission to the bar.[69] People were specially invited to join the bar by the local bureau of justice. Retired officials, government employees, and policemen were frequently invited to join the bar in order to meet the rising demand for lawyers.[70] Additionally, anyone with

> at least a junior college education in law and at least two years of work experience in a law related job; anyone with legal training and work experience in the courts of procuracy; or anyone with a university degree in any subject who underwent legal training and was able to demonstrate legal ability was eligible for admission to the bar.[71]

This imprecise description of who was qualified for admission to the bar had two consequences. First, it kept lawyers weak vis-à-vis the state. As long as admission to the bar was predicated on vaguely defined experiences or, worse yet, the invitation of the government, lawyers would never develop the sense that their membership in the bar was based on their own merit. Instead, it was based on the caprice of the government. This left lawyers with a sense of indebtedness, reliance, and subservience to the state. The second consequence of the loosely worded definition of who was eligible for admission to the bar was a blurry distinction between a lawyer and a nonlawyer advocate. If a license was the only thing that fundamentally distinguished lawyers from other citizens, then it was quite reasonable to assume that there might be people without licenses who would be equally effective or superior advocates. Indeed, there were many such individuals. Although technically an individual had to possess a lawyer's license in order to provide representation in court, nonlawyer advocates termed "rice-roots lawyers" proliferated in response to an environment of rapid growth in demand for legal services and a propensity toward corrupt behavior in the courts.[72] The presence of rice-roots lawyers would later pose several considerable challenges in terms of regulation and standardization of lawyers.

Although the gradual privatization of the legal profession opened up new opportunities for lawyers, it also created animus between lawyers and the *gongjianfa*. Throughout the entire process of privatization, while lawyers increasingly adopted the role of private-sector entrepreneurs, judges and prosecutors remained state employees. As such, their salaries increased along the same schedule as all other civil servants'. Lawyers, former civil servants themselves, grew progressively wealthier as the market responded to growing demands for their services. Lawyers soon left their former comrades behind in terms of wealth. In terms of power, however, the judges and prosecutors retained a large advantage over lawyers. As government employees, the judges and prosecutors were a part of the system. They had access to all of the resources of the government, valuable contacts with officials in other departments, as well as the protection that comes with official status. And, ultimately, the judges determined the outcome of each case. The lawyers, who used to enjoy the benefits of being system insiders, increasingly had to deal with challenges independently. The lawyers were keenly aware of the power gap that existed between themselves and the *gongjianfa*. However, the *gongjianfa* was equally aware of the wealth gap that existed between themselves and the lawyers. Adding to the animus was the fact that neither judges nor prosecutors had to be educated or licensed as lawyers. This left lawyers jealous of the power of the *gongjianfa*, which they considered unearned and undeserved. In turn, the *gongjianfa* was jealous of the wealth of the lawyers, which they similarly considered unearned and undeserved. This bilateral jealousy created fertile conditions for graft.[73]

An endemic problem emerged with lawyers and judges exchanging wealth for power and vice versa. The problem became so serious that many lawyers began to explicitly charge their clients a graft fee: fees that would be earmarked for bribing judges.[74] Many clients were happy to pay the graft fee. In their conception, a client hires a lawyer to achieve a certain outcome. If the client pays the lawyer, the lawyer is obligated to provide the outcome. It did not rest well upon Chinese sensibilities that the outcome might not be achieved even after the client had paid. In a simple sense, this perspective is quite reasonable. If someone sold you a lamp but the lamp never materialized, you would not tolerate this as an acceptable exchange. In the view prevalent in China in the 1990s, as long as you were willing to pay, your outcome should be guaranteed. Absent from this view is an appreciation of the fact that, worldwide, lawyers are paid not to provide an outcome but to provide legal services which may or may not produce the desired outcome. Where this nuance is not appreciated, it is easy to understand how a client could feel comfortable, even enthusiastic, about paying a graft fee. Either way, the client is trying to purchase an outcome. In fact, there existed some contemporary sentiment that it would be more efficient for the client to go directly to the judge to bribe him, cutting out the middleman. Lawyers in this view were not seen as possessors of valuable knowledge of law, and the courtroom was not seen as an arena for competing interpretations of the law. Rather, lawyers were seen as purveyors of influence, and the courtroom was viewed as a platform for mobilizing influence and money.

In 1995 the National People's Congress passed the Judges Law, which is still in effect today.[75] The Judges Law stipulated a set of minimum credentials for holding judgeships and formally articulated the channels for hiring and firing judges. These credentials include having "fine political and professional quality" and being "good in conduct."[76] The credentials also include having worked for at least two years in the case of graduates from university law programs or graduates from nonlaw university programs with a professional knowledge of law. For seated judges who did not possess these qualifications prior to the implementation of the Judges Law, specialized courses were created to give them the necessary training.

The Judges Law invests the people's congress of each level of government with the authority to elect and remove the president of the people's court at the corresponding level.[77] The president is then responsible for nominating the vice presidents, members of the judicial committees, chief judges and associate chief judges, and judges. All nominations must be approved by the standing committee of the people's congress at the corresponding level of government.

The Judges Law also established provisions for the annual evaluation of all judges by the court that employs them.[78] An evaluation may result in three different rankings: excellent, competent, and incompetent.

If a judge is deemed incompetent two years in a row, he is subject to dismissal.

In 1996 the National People's Congress passed the Lawyers Law. The Lawyers Law defined lawyers as "professionals providing legal services to society," a marked departure from "state legal workers," as defined by the 1980 Provisional Regulations on Lawyers. The Lawyers Law also created a requirement that all new lawyers pass the bar examination and stipulated that the minimum credentials required to sit for the exam were a junior-college degree in law through a self-study distance-learning program and a one-year internship at an established law firm.[79] These requirements, minimal though they were, promised to greatly aid the process of establishing a common denominator for the bar. However, the Lawyers Law did nothing to bring the rice-roots lawyers into the fold. The Lawyers Law did, however, establish a framework for state-directed pro bono work. Article 42 of the Lawyers Law stipulated that legal-aid cases assigned by the state to a private-sector lawyer become mandatory obligations. This requirement accomplished two things: it created access to lawyers for poor citizens, and it helped to improve the popular perception of lawyers by giving back to the people.

Perhaps the most significant consequence of the Lawyers Law, however, is that it provided lawyers with unprecedented legal rights and protections.[80] For example, it granted criminal defense lawyers the right to meet with their clients before trial. Shocking though it may sound, this right was not articulated prior to 1996, and criminal defense lawyers often only met their clients for the first time when appearing in the courtroom, obviating any possibility of providing effective defense.

The 1996 Lawyers Law, however, was a double-edged sword. Although it provided several rights for lawyers, it also created a formal legal framework that would allow the state to continue to exercise tremendous influence over lawyers. Article 45 of the Lawyers Law states,

> If a lawyer commits any of the following acts, the judicial administration department of the people's government of a province, autonomous region, or municipality directly under the Central Government shall revoke his practice certificate; where the case

constitutes a crime, criminal responsibility shall be pursued according to law: (1) divulging State secrets; (2) bribing a judge, prosecutor, arbitrator or other relevant working personnel or instigating a party to do so; or (3) providing false evidence, concealing important facts or intimidating or inducing another with promise of gain to provide false evidence or conceal important facts.

Given the Chinese government's nebulous definition of the term *state secret*, the first provision of Article 45 creates an enormous field of taboo that could end the career of a lawyer who tried to push the envelope of acceptable discourse.

The second provision makes it illegal to offer bribes. At first, this may sound like a good restriction. However, one must remember that bribery is omnipresent in China.[81] Bribery was a ubiquitous feature in the Chinese legal world at the time that the Lawyers Law was promulgated, and it remains so today. If a popular activity is banned but the prohibited activity does not diminish, then we must conclude that the prohibition is not enforced. If the prohibition is not enforced, we must ask, *what was the motivation for creating the prohibition*? A simpler question to answer is, *what is the consequence of the prohibition*? The consequence is the creation of a legal framework that allows the government to strip lawyers of their licenses for an act in which all lawyers engage. In this light, the provision can be seen as a noose placed around the neck of lawyers in the event that they do something that the government deems unfavorable.

The third provision goes a step further in curtailing the independence and potency of lawyers. The provision makes it illegal for lawyers to provide false evidence. In the event that a defense lawyer's evidence conflicts with a prosecutor's case against the defendant, a very simple litmus test is administered to determine which party has provided the "false" evidence: all evidence provided by the prosecutor is true. This provision, in effect, creates a framework for the state to indict lawyers if they argue too effectively against prosecutors. As a result of these three provisions of the Lawyers Law, lawyers are extremely reluctant to take up cases that might pit them against the state. If they do take on such cases, they are forced to choose between arguing the case in such a way that grants de facto victory to the prosecutor and sacrificing their own careers, or worse.

There is a term in the Chinese language that appears in almost every discussion of law, politics, and business. The term *guanxi* (关系) means connections, relationships, influence, and so on. Someone who is involved in a dispute and has a relationship with a relevant government official is said to have *guanxi*. In many ways, the legal profession in China in the 1990s was understood in these terms. There is a popular pun-laden expression that says *da guansi jiu shi da guanxi* (打官司就是打关系), meaning "to file a lawsuit is to employ *guanxi*." Heavy reliance on relationships, favors, and other human elements in legal matters can pose a threat to the rule of law. This threat will be explored later, in chapter 3, "The Rule of Law." For now, we will consider the interplay between the foregoing expression and popular attitudes toward lawyers.

The attitude toward lawyers that grew popular during the Qing Dynasty remained dominant throughout the successive eras. This attitude regarded lawyers as *litigation tricksters*, hired by foreign interests to trick people out of their money by ensnaring them in a web of litigation. Modern developments added to this perception the element of lawyers profiting based on illegitimate tactics. It also added the element of selfishness as lawyers grew rich relative to their former comrades, the patriotic civil servants who were left behind by the explosive growth of the private sector. Finally, it added the element of lawyers serving a foreign system of ideas, namely private property rights and capitalism, which were fundamentally contrary to everything that had been inculcated in China over generations of struggle for Marxist-Maoist ideals. All of this added to and reinforced the *litigation trickster* perception. Overcoming this intensely negative perception would pose a great challenge for the legal community.

In 1998 the Ministry of Justice transferred to the All China Lawyers Association many of the responsibilities of administering the lawyer's examination.[82] However, the MOJ retained the responsibility of designing the test questions and determining the pass-fail rate.

The process of privatizing the legal profession culminated in 2000 with a campaign designed by the State Council, the head of the administrative branch of the Chinese government, to privatize all remaining law firms. By 2002, Beijing was completely free of state-owned firms.[83] In the same year, a landmark reform was adopted which streamlined the preparatory channels for judges, prosecutors, and lawyers. Starting in 2002, all new judges and prosecutors would have to pass the same bar examination as lawyers.[84] This examination is called the *sifa kaoshi* (司法考试), or "unified judicial examination." A four-year college degree is required to sit for the *sifa kaoshi*. The lawyers who were licensed before 2002 but lacked college degrees were allowed to retain their licenses. The judges who had never been licensed were required to take a series of specialized training courses over a period of years in order to upgrade them to a higher level of functionality. The intention of the *sifa kaoshi* was to increase the standard of education, quality, and professionalism of the next generation of lawyers, judges, and prosecutors. The effectiveness and consequences of this effort will be discussed in detail in a later chapter.

Many commentators have pointed out a variety of problems with the Lawyers Law. In order to allay some of these criticisms, the government promulgated a revised Lawyers Law, which came into effect on June 1, 2008.[85] There was speculation that the new law might give to the bar association a greater degree of independence from the Ministry of Justice, but these hopes were not fulfilled. However, the new law did widen the scope of attorney-client privilege. For example, under the new law, defense lawyers are allowed to meet with their clients after a police interrogation without having to apply for permission, and, according to the law, their confidential conversations will not be recorded by the police. While it remains to be seen whether or not these new rights will be respected in practice, the fact that they have been legitimized through legislation should be taken as a significant measure of progress.

At the outset of the Opening Up and Reform Policy in 1978, there was a great deal of suspicion surrounding the accumulation of wealth. It was not entirely clear that this latter policy would be any different in intent from the Hundred Flowers Campaign. But even if it wasn't a trap, there existed a popular sentiment that accumulating wealth was contrary to all the struggle that China had endured in the name of the revolution. In the thirty years since 1978, the taboo about wealth has subsided.[86] These thirty years have witnessed the passing of the last generation of revolutionaries. These thirty years have seen a fifteenfold increase in China's wealth.[87] As older generations that were scarred by the uncertainties of the early reform days passed and were replaced by newer generations that were raised with the privileges of wealth, the bias against accumulation faded from memory. For the preceding two centuries, lawyers in China had been disdained for their greed. By the beginning of the twenty-first century, greed had lost the stigma of disdain. In its place was a newly acquired aura of virtue. Greed and accumulation formed the logic of the new economy, and lawyers came to be regarded as model actors in that economy. The lawyer's independence, intellect, and billing power earned accolades for the legal profession.

The development of the legal profession in China was a long and extremely treacherous path. After two hundred years of struggle, the profession had finally established its territory and struck a balance with the government. More importantly, the legal profession finally demonstrated to the populace that it could perform functions that were economically beneficial, if not socially beneficial. After two hundred years, the legal profession finally justified its right to exist.

What remains to be seen is whether the legal profession will be able to grow beyond the confines of the narrow role that was accorded it by history. Will lawyers continue to be regulation specialists, as the etymology of the Chinese term suggests? Or will they become something more substantial? The etymology of the Chinese word for *law* is associated with the attributes of principle, leveling, and truth. Will the role of lawyers expand to fill this entire space of meaning? Teasing out the answer to this question will be the task of the succeeding chapters of this book. The remainder of this chapter will be concerned with offering a few final comments on the vast changes that have taken place in the preceding two hundred years of Chinese history.

At the outset of the nineteenth century, China's leaders were still convinced that Chinese civilization was the only civilization in the world. Today, no such perception exists. The greatest thinkers in the Middle Kingdom have been engaged in a protracted and often bloody struggle to redefine China's relationship with the world. If Chinese civilization is not the only civilization, what are its defining features? How does it relate to other civilizations? How should it relate to other civilizations? What does it mean to be Chinese? For that matter, what is the meaning of China? Partial answers are now beginning to emerge. The struggle continues.

At the outset of the nineteenth century, China's leaders were still convinced that the classics contained universal truths equally applicable to the whole of mankind. Today, no such perception exists; the classics have been thoroughly dethroned. This has important implications for the authority structure in China, in the sense of both moral authority and governmental authority. The classics defined morality for Chinese civilization. In the postclassics age, there is no clearly accepted source of moral authority, nor are there universally accepted methods for discovering, articulating, and evaluating morality. This has practical consequences for governance. Pervasive knowledge of the classics and universal acceptance of classical obligations are the forces that truly governed traditional society. As stated earlier, cultural homogeneity ruled, while the state merely reigned. In the postclassics age, cultural homogeneity can no longer rule because it no longer exists. From this, it is understood that the ongoing experimentations of the Chinese state are no less than forays into the first true government of China, the first Chinese state which not only reigns but also rules. Emphasis should be placed upon the word *experimentation*. There have been disruptions and bumps along the way, and there will surely be more to come. Some of the bumps are minor. Some are rather substantial. The minor bumps should not be overstated by dragon-slayers, and the substantial bumps should not be trivialized by panda-huggers. Small or large, all of the bumps and disruptions should be understood as reasonable setbacks to a governmental undertaking, the magnitude of which the world has never seen: ruling the largest nation in the world after, above, and beyond the mandate of heaven.

CHAPTER 3

THE RULE OF LAW

Most of the discussion in this book is narrowly focused on the topic of Chinese lawyers. What is the point? Unless you're doing business in China, or otherwise interacting with Chinese lawyers, why care? The answer is that lawyers are a part of something larger. Lawyers are intimately related to the structure and order of society. Given that one-fifth of humanity lives in China, we have no choice but to concern ourselves with the structure of Chinese society and how its order impacts the rest of the world. All recent trends underscore the fact that indifference to the Chinese system is a luxury that nobody can afford. Bearing these thoughts in mind, this chapter will attempt to characterize the *rule-of-law* system in China and the role of lawyers in that system.

The rule of law has become the "holy grail" of good governance.[1] In nearly every policy discussion, someone will invariably suggest building the rule of law as the catch-all cure for the problem du jour.[2] But these suggestions are rarely accompanied by a firm understanding of what the rule of law really means, how it is created, and how it is undermined.[3] Most people possess an understanding of the rule of law at an intuitive level, but are unable to articulate the distinctions between rule of law, liberty, and democracy. In order to bring the concept of rule of law into a discussion about China, we must first separate the wheat from the chaff. Once this is done and a deeper understanding of the concept has been achieved, we can proceed to evaluate the current status of the rule of law in China, analyze the relationship between the rule of law and the role of lawyers, and compare the development of the rule of law in China with its historical development in the West. Taken together, all of these pieces will help to form an understanding of the status and future of the rule of law and lawyers in China.

WHAT IS THE RULE OF LAW

First, we must make a distinction between the often befuddled concepts of *democracy*, *liberty*, and *rule of law*. The concept of *democracy* is the easiest of the three to define. Democracy, quite simply, is "a form of government in which supreme power is vested in the people and exercised directly by them or by their elected agents under a free electoral system."[4] The concept of *liberty* is slightly more difficult to define. *Democracy* and *liberty* are often confused as interchangeable or interdependent concepts because they are so frequently found together. But this is not an accurate understanding of the relationship. Not only are they separate concepts, they are actually opposites. America's founding fathers wrote extensively about the threat to liberty arising from unchecked democracy.[5] Whereas democracy vests sovereignty in the people, liberty vests sovereignty in the individual. Whereas democracy is about protecting the people from oppression by individuals, liberty is about protecting individuals from oppression by the people.[6] Recognizing this distinction, we are still left with the task of defining what is meant by the word *liberty*. French Enlightenment philosopher Charles de Montesquieu wrote that "liberty is a right of doing whatever the law permits."[7] In other words, liberty is the right to do whatever the law does not specifically prohibit. This definition is attractive for its simplicity, but it leaves something to be desired. What if the law specifically gives permission to engage in a morally reprehensible act, such as the murder of a Jew in Hitler's Germany? Given that the act is specifically permitted by the law, could one engage in the act without undermining liberty? This difficult question suggests that there is something more to liberty than what the law does and does not permit. Some things are wrong even if they are legal, and some things are right even if they are not legal. In a pluralistic society composed of many cultures and values, it is difficult to make a determination of what is right and wrong, and even more difficult to sculpt the law to the contours of that determination. Although these issues add layers of complexity to Montesquieu's formulation, his formulation is clearly an indispensable component of any functional definition of *liberty*. Liberty simply could not exist in an environment wherein citizens were punished for doing things that the law did not prohibit, so we will take this as the basis for our definition of liberty.

The last term to define is *the rule of law*. As mentioned earlier, most people are not able to articulate the exact meaning of the term. This is largely attributable to the fact that there is no universally accepted definition, even among scholars.[8] There is a general agreement that the phrase *rule of law* describes a scenario in which the law guides the behavior of citizens.[9] However, there is substantial disagreement about what exactly that means and how it is achieved.[10] In order to treat the question of what it means, we shall examine the two major theories of the rule of law. Afterwards, we shall answer the question of how it is achieved by examining the three themes of the rule of law.

There are two major theories of the rule of law and a plethora of minor offshoots and variations. The first theory is called the *formal theory* of the rule of law and the second is called the *substantive theory* of the rule of law. The formal theory takes Montesquieu's conception of liberty as its foundation and adds the requirement that laws must be prospective, general, clear, public, and relatively stable.[11] *Prospectivity* means that laws apply only to the events that occur after their promulgation and never to events that occurred before their promulgation.[12]

> The qualities of generality, certainty, clarity, and prospectivity are all connected to the nature of rules. Generality is an aspect of what

it means to be a "rule," in contrast to a particular "order." That is the essential difference between following a rule or taking an ad hoc action, or making a context-specific decision. Uncertain or unclear rules have limited efficacy in guiding behavior.[13]

If citizens enjoy liberty and laws are prospective, general, clear, public, and stable, then it is said that *formal legality* exists.[14] Formal legality is all about predictability. Friedrich Hayek, the Austrian Nobel Prize–winning economist, articulated a vision of the rule of law that was based largely on formal legality:

> Nothing distinguishes more clearly conditions in a free country from those in a country under arbitrary government than the observance in the former of the great principles known as the Rule of Law. Stripped of all technicalities, this means that government in all its actions is bound by rules fixed and announced beforehand—rules which make it possible to foresee with fair certainty how the authority will use its coercive powers in given circumstances and to plan one's individual affairs on the basis of this knowledge.[15]

This description encapsulates the formal theory of the rule of law.

The substantive theory of the rule of law starts with formal legality and goes beyond, to stake out a broader space of ideals. While the formal theory is only concerned with the attributes of the law that make it predictable, the substantive theory is also concerned with the attributes of the law that make it just, moral, and fair.[16] Thus, the substantive theory is concerned with features such as equality. To distinguish between the formal theory and the substantive theory, imagine a system of laws that mandated class differences and articulated differing rights and obligations to members of the different classes. As long as those rights and obligations are articulated in a prospective, general, clear, public, and stable manner, then this system would provide predictability despite the fact that it would not provide fairness.

We have answered the question of *what the rule of law means* by examining the two major theories. Now we shall treat the question of *how the rule of law is achieved* by examining the following three themes, each of which is commonly found in most explanations of the rule of law.[17]

The first theme is *government limited by law*. This means that the government recognizes the confines of its power to legislate—some things are off limits. It also means that the government is bound by the law that it legislates. This presents an interesting dilemma. If the government is the source of the law, how can it be bound by the law? If the interests of the government come into conflict with the dictates of the law, does not the government have the power to modify the law to conform to its interests? If the government reshapes the law to conform to its interests, then the law will be perceived as nothing more than the transient will of the powerful over the weak. On the other hand, if the government abides by the law that it legislates regardless of how its interests are impacted, then the law will be perceived as legitimate. If the law is perceived as legitimate, then most people will endeavor to obey most of the laws most of the time. On the other hand, if the law is perceived as illegitimate, people will feign appearances of obedience only when it is necessary to do so in order to avoid punishment.

The second theme common to most explanations of the rule of law is *formal legality*. As explained earlier, this means that citizens are only bound by laws which are declared publicly, prospectively, generally, clearly, and stably. This provides businesses and citizens with "predictability and reliability in the enforcement of contractual and property rights as a means to calculate the anticipated benefits of commercial transaction and to secure the fruits of their enterprise."[18] Without a reliable calculation of the anticipated benefits or costs of a given transaction, a rational person would not enter into any sort of agreement more than an arm's length away. More fundamentally, though, an individual cannot possibly meet the obligations of the law if he is not able to understand what obligations are expected of him.

The third theme common to most explanations of the rule of law is a distinction between *the rule of law* and *the rule of man*. This implies that legal decisions must not be based on the outlook of the individual making the decision, but rather, on established principles of jurisprudence. In other words, decisions must be impersonal. This, too, presents an interesting dilemma. Even if a decision maker intends to rely on jurisprudential concepts, he can only access those concepts through the lens of personal interpretation. Therefore, any application of those concepts will be colored by his outlook, obviating any possibility of truly impersonal decision making. This dilemma is unavoidable, but it can be minimized through careful consideration of what sorts of people should be placed in positions of authority to make consequential decisions. According to Professor Brian Tamanaha of St. John's University, "final say in the interpretation and application of the law properly rests with the judiciary…because no other government official undergoes [the] necessary transformation in which the subjective individual is replaced with the objective judge."[19] The transformation of which he speaks begins with a rigorous legal education, followed by a clerkship and years of employment in law. After so many years of deeply contemplating legal problems, it is hoped that judges

> learn not only to see issues from many sides, but, in so doing, also learn to cultivate the art of being simultaneously sympathetic and rigorous, and to understand that politics, and, indeed life generally, prize the art of blending that which is ideal with that which is practical.[20]

This unique perspective enables the judiciary to minimize the influence of personal views in decision making. This is tremendously important, for if personal views were allowed to influence decision making, then the outcome of each case would be determined largely by who was appointed to make the decision. A case could be decided one day by one person, and an identical case could be decided differently the next day, all depending on who was presiding that day. In such a scenario, the attribute of predictability for which the law is so highly prized would be eviscerated.

The three themes explained above are government limited by law, formal legality, and a distinction between the rule of law and the rule of man. These three themes are found in most explanations of the rule of law. Without the conditions that they describe, the law will be ineffective in guiding the behavior of citizens. It should be noted that these conditions are not particular to any political system. There is nothing inherently Western about them; they have been successfully cultivated in non-Western polities. There is nothing inherently democratic about them.[21] In fact, one of the greatest oracles of the Communist Party, E. P. Thompson, once declared the rule of law to be "an unqualified human good."[22] The rule of law could be cultivated in autocracy at least as well as, if not better than, in a democracy. One could imagine an enlightened autocrat who promulgates laws that meet the criteria of formal legality, who accepts those laws as a binding obligation upon himself, and who provides for the adjudication of disputes substantially free of personal bias. Such laws would be effective in guiding behavior. There is nothing that precludes the rule of law from existing without democracy. Ironically, however, democracy cannot exist without the rule of law. If the rule of law is not respected, then democratically established laws will be ineffective, resulting in anarchy.

Rule of Law in the Middle Kingdom

Now that the full anatomy of the rule of law has been laid bare, let us attempt to characterize the rule of law in the Middle Kingdom. It is the uncontroversial position of this book that the rule of law in China is weak. This position will be justified from two approaches: *cause* and *effect*. What is meant by *effect* is the inability of the law to guide the behavior of the citizenry. What is meant by *cause* is the shortcoming of each of the three themes of the rule of law. Let us first explore the effect and then explain the cause.

Chinese law is ineffective in guiding the behavior of the people. This will be established by examining several areas of law in which there is a widespread divergence between the demands of the law and the behavior of the people. Apologists will claim that *there are people who fall short of the demands of the law in every country, so the fact that this is also present in China proves nothing*. But this raises the question, how many people must disobey the law before it may be said that the law is not obeyed?

What percentage of the populace must contravene the law before it may be said that the law is not in control? The task of answering these questions shall be left to the reader. The task at hand is to present the reader with evidence of a broad pattern of behavior in which the demands of the law are unmet. This pattern of behavior is conspicuously evident in all areas of endeavor, beginning with the most primary of human activities, sex. It is a crime to engage in the act of prostitution in the People's Republic of China, as well as to hire the services of a prostitute, but prostitution is nevertheless extremely common.[23] It is difficult to say exactly how common prostitution is, or how many prostitutes there are, as it is difficult to measure the extent of any illicit activity. Figures range from 3 million to 20 million prostitutes nationwide. Professor Yang Fan, a prominent economist at the China University of Politics and Law, has estimated that prostitution accounts for a full 6 percent of China's gross domestic product![24] This figure is quite high and quite startling. Perhaps the only thing more startling is the pervasiveness of marital infidelity. The first chapter of the Marriage Law of the People's Republic of China repeatedly specifies the requirement for monogamy within marriages.[25] Nonetheless, infidelity is rampant. There are luxury compounds, known as *er nai cun* (二奶村), or "second wives' luxury compounds, that exist solely for the purpose of housing mistresses.[26] The greatest evidence of disregard for the marriage law is found in the text of the Eight Prohibitions, a set of anticorruption regulations passed in 2007.[27] The regulations specify certain "individuals with special relationships" who must be subjected to additional scrutiny if they enter into business dealings with government officials. "Individuals with special relationships" is defined as "individuals who share close familial relations including mistresses with state officials." The fact that the regulations conceive of a special category for mistresses, and that this category is included as a subset of familial relations, belies the extent of marital infidelity in China. The size of the prostitution industry and the extent of marital infidelity are both good examples of the divergence between the demands of the law and the behavior of the people.

The divergence is also manifested through rampant violations of employment law. The 1994 China Labor Law and its attendant regulations stipulate that it is illegal to employ a child younger than sixteen years old.[28] It is also illegal to employ an individual without offering compensation, or to force an individual to work against his or her will. Yet all of these prohibitions are frequently ignored. In April 2008, police in Guangdong Province raided a child-labor ring that had kidnapped scores of children between the ages of thirteen and fifteen from the Liangshan area of Sichuan Province and forced them to work physically demanding jobs in coastal cities, often without pay.[29] It is important to mention that the government only took action after the child-labor ring was discovered and publicized by an investigative newspaper called the *Southern Metropolis*. An editorial that was published after the raid questioned, "Since journalists could discover the facts by secret interviews in a few days, how could the labor departments show no interest in it and ignore it for such a long time?"[30] This is a very important question which will be revisited in a later section. For now, we will address the commonness of violations of this nature. According to Professor Hu Xingdou, an economist at the Beijing Institute of Technology, "the Liangshan child labor case is quite typical. China's economy is developing at a fascinating speed, but often at the expense of laws, human rights and environmental protection."[31]

Professor Hu at once suggests the regularity with which labor laws are violated and also points out another area of law which is ineffective in guiding the behavior of citizens: environmental law. In 2007 the Organization for Economic Cooperation and Development released a report that assessed the impact of China's environmental policies since 1990.[32] The report praised China's successful accomplishments in modernizing its environmental laws and regulations, but concluded that the laws were by and large ineffective in curbing undesirable behaviors such as pollution, emissions, and exorbitant energy use. According to the report, the laws were ineffective due to an "implementation gap" at the local level.[33] The reader should notice a pattern emerging between marital law, employment law, and environmental law. In each case, there is a substantial gap between what the law demands and what is actually done. Two additional areas of law will be examined to further demonstrate this point: product safety law and intellectual property law.

The Product Quality Law of the People's Republic of China came into force on September 1, 1993, and was subsequently amended on July 8, 2000.[34] The Food Hygiene Law of the People's Republic of China was promulgated on October 30, 1995.[35] Together, these two laws addressed a wide range of potential hazards that might arise in the manufacture and processing of food and products, such as lead poisoning, chemical content, toxic substances, defective parts, and so on.[36] The two laws also regulate production facilities, packaging, and transportation of goods, all with the aim of ensuring safety.[37] The two laws also make provisions about inspection and quality assurance.[38] It would seem that they covered all the bases. Despite the comprehensive breadth of both pieces of law, however, they proved ineffective in guiding the behavior of manufacturers and food-processing companies toward responsible practices. The figure below represents the number of product recalls that the U.S. Consumer Product Safety Commission (CPSC) has issued since the beginning of 2001 for each of several countries. The countries included are America's top five trading partners, which includes China as well as Brazil, India, and Pakistan, in order to provide points of comparison that are more similar to China in terms of developmental circumstances.

On its face, this data simply shows that the CPSC recalls more products from China than from any of the other countries shown. Chinese apologists often claim that the Chinese product-quality problem perceived by American consumers is really a function of China's status as America's factory floor and China's status as a developing country. But because four of the other countries shown here are also large trading partners of America, the Chinese problem cannot be explained away as a function of China's large volume of trade with America. And because three of the other countries shown are also developing countries, the Chinese problem also cannot be explained away as a function of China's developmental circumstances. The truth is that the Chinese figures are whole orders of magnitude too great to be explained away by these factors.

In September 2007, as the attention of the international media focused in on this problem, Chinese authorities announced a nationwide campaign

FIGURE 3. CPSC recalls by country since 2001.

	China	Canada	Mexico	Japan	India	Pakistan	Brazil
2001	11	0	0	1	0	0	0
2002	67	5	0	1	0	1	1
2003	80	4	3	2	6	0	0
2004	132	7	11	3	5	1	1
2005	154	6	9	9	1	1	1
2006	172	11	11	14	3	3	3
2007	302	8	7	8	9	5	5
2008	227	11	7	6	11	1	1
2009	223	3	12	0	10	8	8

Source. Adapted from Consumer Product Safety Commission (2009).
Note. The 2009 figures were calculated by summing the number of recalls that had occurred as of July 29, 2009, and multiplying by 12/7 to produce annualized figures.

to improve quality and safety, headed by Vice Premier Wu Yi.[39] Additionally, Chinese authorities agreed to put food, product, and drug safety on the agenda for the next round of the United States–China Strategic Economic Dialogue (SED), to be held in Beijing in December 2007. The SED yielded two agreements intended to improve the quality and safety of food, manufactured products, and pharmaceutical goods.[40] The agreements were specifically designed to patch the holes in the extant regulatory system. In January 2008, the government declared Vice Premier Wu Yi's four-month-long campaign a success.[41] Among other achievements of the campaign, thousands of unlicensed food-processing plants and illegal underground factories were shut down, and roughly 1,200 licenses were revoked for dangerous drug and medical-equipment companies. Between the achievements of the campaign and the new legal framework adopted at the SED, Beijing was justifiably optimistic when it asserted that *Made in China* was safe again. But that optimism proved unfounded.

On February 1, 2008, the Japanese government announced that more than 175 people had become ill or hospitalized after eating a particular brand of dumplings that had been imported from China.[42] The dumplings were produced by Tianyang Food Processing Ltd., located in Hebei Province. Clinical tests showed that the dumplings were contaminated with insecticide.[43] The Japanese government and private retailers undertook a large recall of Chinese-made food products. Shortly thereafter, American authorities announced that scores of people who had taken the blood thinner heparin had experienced an allergic reaction, low blood pressure, and other serious health complications. More than one thousand incidents were reported, and eighty-one deaths occurred. The U.S. Food and Drug Administration (FDA) traced the supply chain of the heparin back to China.[44] The FDA's investigation found a total of twelve Chinese firms that had sold contaminated heparin to eleven countries: Australia, Canada, China, Denmark, France, Germany, Italy, Japan, the Netherlands, New Zealand, and the United States. In September 2008, it was discovered that the baby formula sold by several Chinese firms was heavily contaminated with melamine, an ingredient which is commonly found in plastic and which is toxic if ingested. More than 300,000 infants fell ill, and six died.[45] Parents all over China were distraught at the realization that none of the baby-formula brands to which they had access were truly safe. One mother lamented,

> I'm just praying there's nothing wrong with my son...We first fed him Sanlu, then stopped because that was reported to be bad quality, then we switched to Yashili, but now there's nothing left. We don't know what's safe anymore and we don't want to take any chances.[46]

Around the same time, French consumers began to complain of furniture imported from China which was reported to cause rashes, allergic reactions, eczema, and infections in hundreds of cases, even sending several consumers to the hospital. The furniture was coated in dimethyl fumarate, an antifungal compound. Although it is common practice to treat furniture with dimethyl fumarate, the furniture in question contained ten times more of the chemical than was normal.[47] In light of all of these anecdotes, it is evident that Chinese producers continue to exhibit a distinct quality problem. As a corollary, we must concede that China's food- and product-safety laws are not effective in guiding producers to adopt safe practices.

China's intellectual property laws are similarly ineffective. Modern concepts of intellectual property rights have circulated in China since at least 1903.[48] In 1982 the Trademark Law of the People's Republic of China was promulgated,[49] followed by the Patent Law in 1984.[50] The concept of copyright was first acknowledged by the law with the promulgation of the General Principles of Civil Law in 1986.[51] Thus, the three principal forms of intellectual property rights had found a legal basis by the end of the 1980s. Over the next quarter-century, these rights were repeatedly updated and amended. However, none of this fine-tuning yielded the result for which it was intended. Intellectual property piracy remains the rule, rather than the exception, in China.

Stories of Chinese piracy are well known. Everyone has heard that you can buy bootlegged DVDs on the streets of Beijing for one dollar, even before the movie has been released in America. As ubiquitous and harmful as this, bootlegged DVDs are hardly the most harmful aspect of China's intellectual property piracy. Much more harmful is the bootlegging of higher-value products such as integrated circuits, computer software, and Web sites. For example, below, there is an image of Facebook, an American social-networking Web site that was created in 2004, followed by an image of Xiaonei, a Chinese social-networking Web site that was created in 2005.[52] Chinese piracy also extends to pharmaceutical drugs, medical devices, cell phones, industrial machines, automobiles, aircraft parts, and even entire factories!

> The Italian press recently reported the case of a machine tool factory in Modena, which was told by one of its regular clients that he had "recently visited your branch in China", which he described as "a replica, right down to the production lines, canteen and lavatories". The manager replied that the Modena firm did not have a branch in China. It had, however, hosted a delegation of Chinese visitors, who, he now recalled, had noted "every last detail" of the factory's layout and facilities.[53]

FIGURE 4. Screen shot of Facebook.

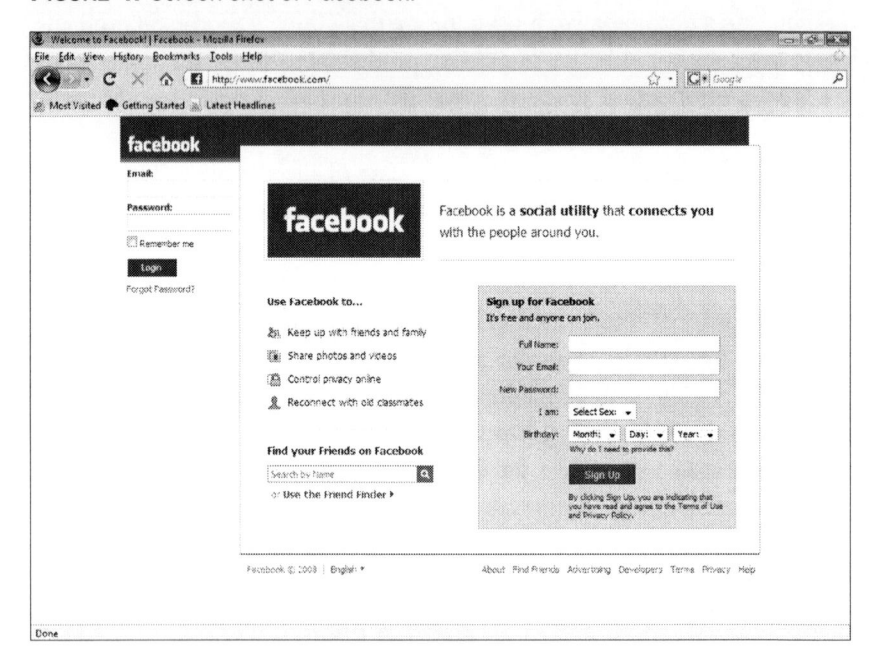

Source. Captured from http://www.facebook.com.

One lawyer from Shanghai spoke to us extensively about his views on intellectual property piracy:

> I work in one of the best law firms in Shanghai, I graduated from one of the top law schools in China, and I have an LLM from the University of Melbourne in Australia. I understand all of the justifications for protecting intellectual property rights, and when my professional duties require, I will do it. But when I want to buy designer clothes or software, realistically, I'm going to buy the pirated copy.[54]

The scale of China's piracy is without parallel. To put it into perspective,

> China currently accounts for approximately 20 percent of the world's population, with 1.3 billion people. This percentage appears to be

FIGURE 5. Screen shot of Xiaonei.

Source. Captured from http://www.xiaonei.com.

proportionately represented in U.S. import statistics, with China accounting for approximately 16 percent of all U.S. imports by value in 2006, yet 81 percent of all counterfeit goods seized [while entering America] that year originated in China.[55]

In 2007 80 percent of counterfeit goods seized while entering American originated in China.[56] "Similarly, while 13.4 percent of total EU imports came from China in 2005, the country accounted for a much larger percentage of counterfeit goods entering the EU at 64 percent."[57]

The U.S. copyright industries estimate that in 2006, 85 percent to 93 percent of all copyrighted material sold in China was pirated, indicating little or no improvement over 2005.[58] Every year, the American Chamber of Commerce in China (ACCC) conducts a survey of member

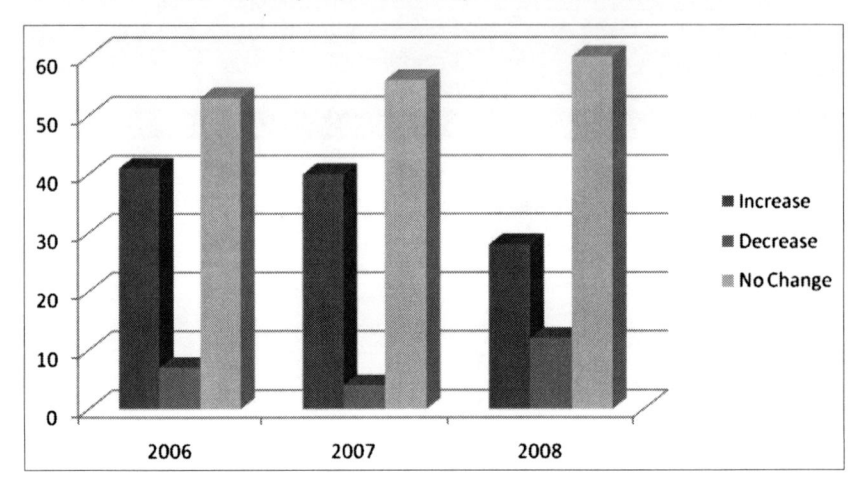

FIGURE 6. Trends in piracy experienced by American companies in China.

Source. Adapted from American Chamber of Commerce in China.

companies. In 2006 the survey indicated that 41 percent of member corporations experienced increases in counterfeits of their goods over the previous year, 7 percent experienced a decrease, and 53 percent experienced no change.[59] In 2007 40 percent experienced an increase, 4 percent experienced a decrease, and 56 percent experienced no change.[60] In 2008 28 percent experienced an increase, 12 percent experienced a decrease, and 60 percent experienced no change.[61]

The most positive spin that one could put on these numbers is that the status quo is becoming more common. This is part of a growing body of data which suggests that conditions in China concerning the protection of intellectual property rights are not improving. We must concede, then, that China's intellectual property laws are not effective in guiding the behavior of Chinese citizens.

Whether one considers marriage law, labor law, environmental law, product safety law, intellectual property law, or any other area of law, the same pattern emerges: there is a wide disparity between what the law demands and what the people do. The law is consistently inconsistent in its ability to guide the behavior of the people. This is the *effect*.

Now let us address the *cause*. The three themes of the rule of law are government limited by law, formal legality, and the distinction between the rule of law and the rule of man. Each of these themes is found to be lacking in China. The first theme, government limited by law, means both that the government abides by the law that it legislates and that the government recognizes limitations to its power to legislate. A brief review of the praxis of the Chinese government will yield the conclusion that the Chinese government is not limited by law in either sense. First, let us ask, does the Chinese government abide by the law that it creates? Professor Pan Wei, an eminent political scientist at Peking University, has written that "it is widely believed within the Communist Party that if the regime falls, corruption will be the most immediate cause."[62] This corruption includes bribery, abuse of power, and outright theft. In 2007, the government, by its own estimate, misused or embezzled nearly $7 billion.[63] Although it is commonly assumed that corruption is only found in the lower ranks, it is, in fact, a pandemic problem that reaches all the way up to the highest echelons of the government. Mr. Chen Liangyu, "who rose through the ranks to become a prominent mayor [of Shanghai], eloquent party boss, and role model for a generation of local officials,"[64] was convicted of corruption in 2007. He had accepted millions of yuan in bribes and "was instrumental in steering billions of Yuan from the city's pension fund into highway and business projects of close associates."[65] If the individuals that comprise the government are serial law violators, then it would be difficult to defend the position that the government, as an entity, abides by the law. The other aspect of government limited by law is governmental recognition of limitations to its own power to legislate. From a postmodernist perspective, the rights of individuals as well as the relationship between the individual and the community, the community and government, and so on, are all culturally specific determinations. If there is no universal determination for where the rights of the government ought to stop and where the rights of the individual ought to begin, how can we make an assessment of the government's willingness to recognize boundaries to its legislative powers? Thankfully, this difficult question can be circumvented through a reference to one of the more absurd laws of the Chinese government. In August of 2007,

> China...banned Buddhist monks in Tibet from reincarnating without government permission. According to a statement issued by the State Administration for Religious Affairs, the law, which goes into effect next month and strictly stipulates the procedures by which one is to reincarnate, is "an important move to institutionalize management of reincarnation."[66]

In the presence of laws such as this, which attempt to subordinate the most ethereal aspects of metaphysics to the government regulation, it is not possible to believe that the government recognizes any sense of limitations to its legislative powers. Therefore, in both senses of the theme, the Chinese government is not limited by law.

The second theme is formal legality. In other words, laws are expressed publicly, prospectively, generally, clearly, and stably in such a way that allows citizens and businesses to "foresee with fair certainty how the authority will use its coercive powers in given circumstances and to plan one's individual affairs on the basis of this knowledge."[67] According to Professor Zhu Yikun, a prominent Chinese legal scholar, "most [Chinese] laws are skeletal...they leave large room for interpretation and clarification by administrative regulations and ministerial rules."[68] Oftentimes, the key parameters of a law will only be alluded to within the text as something to be determined by administrative regulation. For example, the Food Hygiene Law provides that "food shall be nontoxic and harmless, conform to proper nutritive requirements and have appropriate sensory properties such as colour, fragrance and taste."[69] On the plain meaning of this statute, it is not possible to determine what constitutes *nontoxic*, and the requirement that food have an *appropriate* taste is equally unenlightening. Only when read in conjunction with the nutrition standards promulgated by the administrative department of public health under the State Council do any of these terms acquire definition. Thus, the statute relies on administrative regulations for meaning. Unfortunately, reliance on administrative regulations is not conducive to formal legality. Administrative regulations vary from province to province and county to county. Furthermore, administrative regulations are subject to change without the same sort of due process that would be required to change the law. As a result, it is very difficult to maintain a full awareness of what is required and what is allowed by the regulations at any given time in any given place, let alone over a period of time or across the country. Thus, Chinese laws do not possess the attribute of stability required by formal legality because they are subject to change. They do not possess the attribute of clarity required by formal legality because an understanding of legal obligations is often not clearly forthcoming from textual analysis, but is only available by consulting numerous bureaucracies. Finally, formal legality requires the attribute of generality. Chinese laws are simultaneously general and nongeneral. They are general in the sense that they are ostensibly equally applicable to all situations. They do not contain particular orders that are only applicable in certain cases, nor do they offer context-specific decisions. But they are nongeneral in the sense that they vest so much authority in administrators and bureaucrats who do make context-specific decisions. For all of these reasons, the tendency of the Chinese legal system to rely on administrative regulations to supply the content of the law is not conducive to formal legality.

The third theme is a distinction between the rule of law and the rule of man. This entails making legal decisions based on principles of jurisprudence rather than on personal outlook. Obviously, this requires that individuals who are empowered to make legal decisions be trained in jurisprudence. In this regard, China misses the mark. According to Professor Andrew Mertha, an expert on the Chinese government at Cornell University, the court system "is far from the default conflict resolution and law enforcement mechanism in China today."[70] Rather, the default conflict-resolution and law-enforcement mechanism is the administrative bureaucracy. For example, Professor Mertha explains that "an overwhelming amount of the activity surrounding the enforcement of IPR [intellectual property rights] takes place outside the courtroom and in the

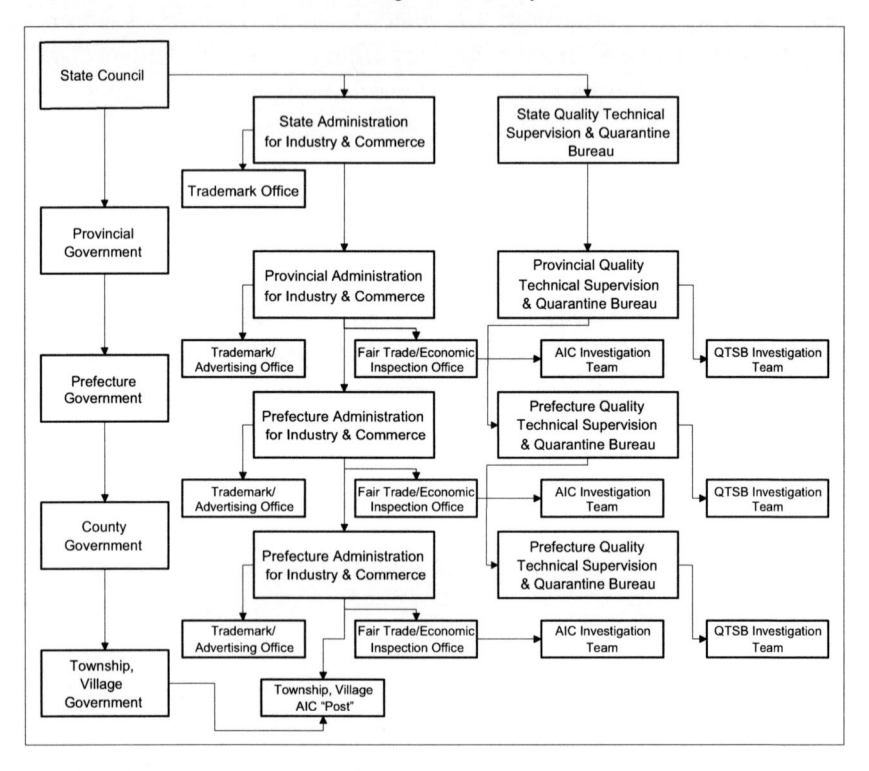

FIGURE 7. China's anticounterfeiting bureaucracy.

Source. Adapted from Trade Lawyers Advisory Group (2007).

halls of China's complex cluster of IPR enforcement bureaucracies."[71] The bureaucracies of which Professor Mertha speaks are depicted by the following figures.[72]

Reliance upon administrative bureaucracies for interpreting and enforcing the law undermines the rule of law in three ways: unpredictability, corruption, and inefficiency. First, bureaucrats are not trained in law. When a petition is brought before a bureaucrat, he can only make a decision based on the facts at hand and his personal outlook, opinions, and predispositions. As these latter three factors will vary substantially from person to person, decisions will vary substantially from bureaucrat to bureaucrat, even when the facts are identical. Under these conditions, the predictability for which the law is so highly prized will be eliminated. Second, reliance upon administrative bureaucracies for interpreting and enforcing the law is inherently conducive to corruption. Because of the architecture of China's public-finance system, local governments are highly dependent upon tax revenue for their functioning. A large portion of this revenue comes from selling business licenses and permits to local enterprises. Thus, the financial solvency of the local government is tied up in the prosperity of the local economy. In some cases, this creates a conflict of interests. Administrative bureaucracies, organs of the local government, are often reluctant to take actions that will reduce or eliminate tax revenues coming from local business that are engaged in counterfeiting, contribute to environmental degradation, or otherwise violate the law.[73] Admittedly, court personnel are also employees of the government, so there is a potential for a similar conflict of interest among judges. However, there are additional layers of insulation between the judges and the local government which make the judiciary less susceptible to this problem.[74] The third and final problem with relying upon administrative bureaucracies for interpreting and enforcing the law is inefficiency. The messy thicket of bureaucracies depicted above is not nimble enough to create effective enforcement. The bureaucracies are too centralized, resources are too scarce, and the incentives acting on bureaucrats do not provide adequate motivation to go out and pursue violators. The salary of a government bureaucrat is more or less constant, regardless of performance. Even the most sophisticated bonus system imaginable cannot simulate the incentives of the market. By contrast, a system of courts and lawyers is decentralized, the resources required to find and organize the facts of each case are supplied by litigants, and the incentives acting on lawyers are such that the more cases they bring to trial, the more money they make. To illustrate this point, let us return to the question asked by the *Southern Metropolis* in response to the Liangshan child-labor case: "Since journalists could discover the facts by secret interviews in a few days, how could the labor departments show no interest in it and ignore it for such a long time?"[75] The answer is that the labor departments have no incentive to go out into the field and pursue violators of the law. By contrast, lawyers are motivated by the prospect of personal gain to fan out and pursue every opportunity to profit by prosecuting violations of the law. If this pursuit is maintained, it will result in the creation of a culture of liability. Over time, this culture becomes so thick and tangible that a whole range of violations disappears from the consciousness of the people as viable courses of action. The culture of liability becomes the principal agent of enforcement, rather than lawyers, judges, or bureaucrats. The culture of liability provides for immediate and omnipresent enforcement. Administrative bureaucracies are simply not able to create a comparable culture. Thus, as long as interpretation and enforcement of the law is carried out in the halls of the bureaucracy rather than in the halls of the court, the rule of man will prevail over the rule of law.

In our review of the three themes of the rule of law in China, each theme is found lacking. This is the *cause* of the weakness of the rule of law in China. The *effect*, as explained earlier, is that the capacity of the law to guide the behavior of the people is limited. The limitations vary from area to area, depending on the local conditions. The rule of law is much more robust in large cities like Beijing and Shanghai than it is in small towns in the interior. Given the vastness of China and all of its regional variations, it is difficult to describe the entire country with a single characterization. But to the extent that this can be done, the rule of law in the Middle Kingdom is found to be weak.

Asking When by Asking Why

It is nice to know that the rule of law is weak, but what most people want to know is, *when will it become strong*? When will the law become effective in guiding the behavior of the people? In order to ask when, we must first ask why. It has already been established that the three themes of the rule of law are lacking in China. Now we endeavor to ask why. It has already been established that Chinese law is too general to support the conditions of formal legality. Now we ask why. It has already been established that the primacy of the bureaucracies over the courts prioritizes the rule of man over the rule of law. Now we ask why. We seek to explain all of the observed phenomena within a single, cogent framework.

There is a new field of comparative law, called leximetrics, which offers promising answers to these questions. Initial leximetric research has shown that laws in some countries are consistently written in a substantially longer fashion than identical laws in other countries.[76] One might be inclined to assume that this is due to linguistic differences—some languages are more verbose than others. But even after controlling for linguistic differences, it has been shown that laws in some countries are simply longer than the same laws in other countries. It has also been shown that the countries with longer laws tend to have longer constitutions, longer contracts, and longer civil-court decisions. Finally, it has been shown that the countries with longer legal instruments tend to have larger lawyer populations. Leximetrics seeks to explain all of these observations, and begins with two assumptions. The first assumption is that more words are needed to specify more details. Therefore, legal length is taken as a proxy for legal specificity. The second assumption is

> that drafters of any legal document seek to control the behavior of interpreters of the document…More specific obligations help control behavior by limiting interpretive discretion. It follows that greater divergence of interests between drafters and interpreters should lead to longer legal texts.[77]

In other words, if the drafters and the interpreters are like-minded, then there is no need for the drafters to specify details because it can be assumed that laws will be interpreted in the way that the drafters intended. Under these circumstances, specifying details would unnecessarily tie the hands of the drafters, limiting future freedom of action. In the event that a rogue interpreter disagrees with the consensus of the drafters, the drafters may have recourse through nonlegal channels, such as administrative bureaucracies. Additionally, if the coalition of drafters that produced the original law remains in power, then they can easily issue corrective legislation to clarify how the original law was meant to be interpreted. The mere threat of corrective legislation will deter most rogue interpreters from expressing disagreement with the drafters. Of course, the threat of corrective legislation is only credible as long as it is expected that the coalition will remain in power. Similarly, drafting nonspecific legislation is only logical as long as it is expected that the coalition will remain in power. If the dominance of a coalition is in jeopardy, then drafters will write very specific legislation in order to hedge against the possibility that future interpreters from another coalition might apply an interpretation that is unfavorable to the present coalition.

In order to test this hypothesis, professors Robert Cooter of the University of California, Berkeley, and Thomas Ginsburg of the University of Chicago performed a quantitative analysis of the length of legal instruments in many countries and the strength of each country's dominant political party relative to the second-strongest political party. Their analysis confirmed that the stronger the dominant political party is, the less specific legislation will be. They went on to explain the relationship between specific legislation and large lawyer populations. The more specific legislation becomes, the more difficult it becomes to understand what the law is saying without a specialized legal education. In order to minimize liability, businesses and individuals must then consult lawyers to ascertain the legal obligations and expectations in their field of endeavor. Thus, in countries with specific legislation, there is greater demand for lawyers' services. On the other hand, in countries with nonspecific legislation, it is easier for a layperson to interpret the law, and as a result, there is less demand for lawyers' services. As long as government regulation of the profession is not restrictive, large or small lawyer populations will develop as a natural response to demand.

Although China is found lacking in the three themes of the rule of law, the leximetric perspective is a cause for optimism. This perspective suggests that China may be making improvements in the area of formal legality. In China in 1949, there was near-perfect solidarity within the Communist Party.[78] There was universal acceptance of fundamental political ideas such as the evil nature of capitalists and Americans, the amiability of the Soviet Union, the infallibility of Mao, and the divinity of Marx. Resting on this solidarity, between 1949 and 1954, drafters felt very comfortable delegating most of the details of the law to administrative bureaucracies. Thus, the proportion of laws to administrative regulations was miniscule.[79] However, as time went on, solidarity gradually gave way to diversity of opinions within the party. As party members of different perspectives coalesced around cliques and interest groups, the prospect of unfavorable future interpretations reduced drafters' comfort with relying on administrative bureaucracies. Thus, by 2000, the proportion of laws to administrative regulations had grown to nearly one-half.

Additional insight can be gleaned from the history of the Chinese constitution. Since the founding of the People's Republic of China in 1949, there have been four constitutions. The first constitution was promulgated in 1954,[80] to be replaced by the 1975 constitution,[81] followed by the 1978 constitution [82] and, finally, the 1982 constitution.[83] Since 1982, the constitution has been amended. A comparison of the word count of each constitution shows uninterrupted growth in length from 1975

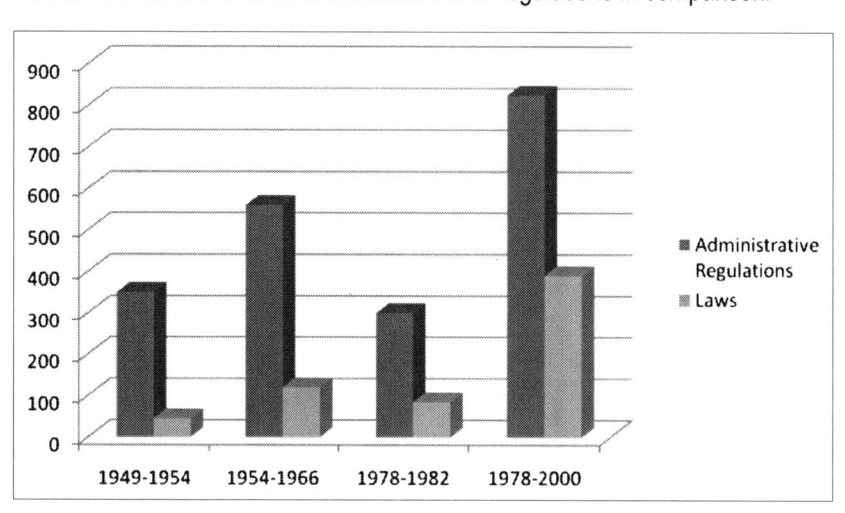

FIGURE 8. Number of laws and administrative regulations in comparison.

Source. Adapted from Zhu (2003).

until 2004. However, length contracted from 1954 to 1975. The explanation for this contraction is that the 1975 constitution was drafted at the tail end of the Cultural Revolution. Acting on the belief that the Party was plagued by capitalists and rightists, one of Mao's chief motives in launching the Cultural Revolution was to purge dissidents.[84] During this time, even thinking thoughts that contravened the will of Mao was an act of considerable peril. Needless to say, the threat of rogue interpreters openly defying Mao was not a source of concern. Thus, the drafters of the 1975 constitution felt perfectly comfortable leaving most of the details out of the law.

As explained earlier, leximetrics maps a relationship between the specificity of legal instruments and the growth of lawyer populations. In conformity with the predictions of leximetric theory, there were only a handful of lawyers in China in 1954, there were no lawyers in China in 1975, and by 2004, the lawyer population exceeded one hundred thousand.

As the Chinese constitution has grown in length, so too have China's intellectual property laws. The Trademark Law of the People's Republic

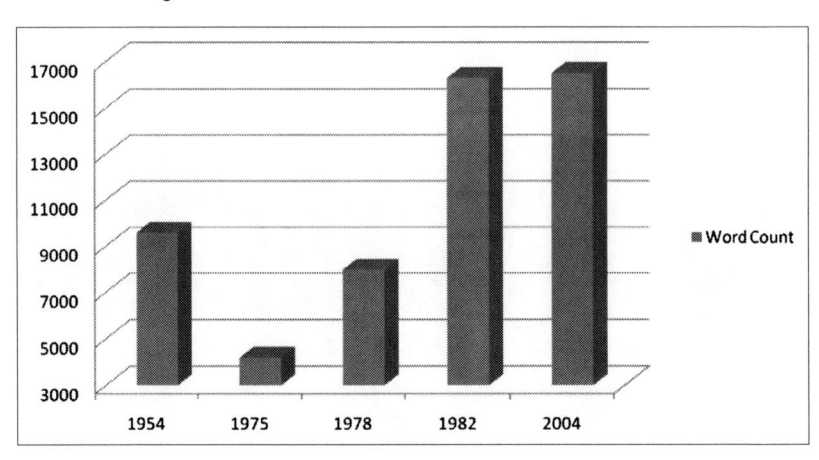

FIGURE 9. Length of Chinese constitutions as a function of time.

Source. Adapted from http://www.chinalawinfo.com.

of China was promulgated in 1982.[85] An amended version of the Trademark Law was promulgated in 1993,[86] and another in 2001.[87] The Patent Law of the People's Republic of China was promulgated in 1984.[88] An amended version of the Patent Law was promulgated in 1992,[89] and another in 2008.[90] The figure below shows each of these laws and their respective word counts. There is an evident trend toward increasing length and, thus, increasing specificity.

Based on the preliminary data, it appears that legal instruments in China are becoming more specific as the party splinters into cliques and interest groups. This bodes well for formal legality, the growth of the bar, and the rule of law. The prospects for the future appear to depend on cultivating greater diversity of opinions within the Party, or at least avoiding stultifying them.

Backward Looking Forward

Having achieved a thorough understanding of the anatomy of the rule of law as well as its present status in China, it would be informative to

Figure 10. Length of Chinese patent and trademark laws as a function of time.

	Year	Words
Trademark Law	1982	1,860
	1993	2,142
	2001	4,843
	Year	**Words**
Patent Law	1984	3,765
	1992	4,000
	2008	4,820

Source. Adapted from http://www.chinalawinfo.com.

review how the rule of law came about in the West. More than two thousand years ago, Rome's greatest orator, Marcus Tullius Cicero, opined that "we are slaves to the law so that we may be free."[91] Even earlier, ancient Greek philosophers identified the rule of law as a trait of the ideal state.[92] Despite the early origin of the rule of law as an ideal in European antiquity, the rule of law as a reality did not emerge until relatively recently. Nonetheless, the fact that it emerged at all is quite astounding. As great a challenge as it is for a contemporary state to cultivate the rule of law, which requires solving the dilemma of subordinating the ruler to his own rules, it must have been a far greater challenge to solve this dilemma in the darkness of generations past. It is likened to the difficulty of synthesizing a complex medical compound in a laboratory under the careful instruction of a scientist, compared to the unlikelihood of the compound growing spontaneously in nature. What made Europe predisposed to the rule of law were the hidden forces that governed premodern European society. These forces are natural law, customary law, and divine law. *Natural law* is the concept that there exists a law inscribed in the fabric of nature which is inherently valid everywhere and at all times. This concept was common currency among European philosophers since Plato.[93] *Customary law* is the product of generations of inherited customs and practices which traditionally governed exchanges between persons.[94] Because customary law is built on tradition, it reflects the collected expectations of all members of the group. As a result, customary law is very effective in maintaining order. *Divine law* is the concept that there exists a law that comes from God, or a god. In the European context, divine law was a product of Judeo-Christian religion. Divine law was particularly strong in premodern Europe because of the prominent role of the Roman Catholic Church in civil government. The common thread between natural law, customary law, and divine law is that each of these systems was thought to exist above humanity, their precepts out of the reach of meddling monarchs. No matter how much power a king might claim, he could never claim the power to alter the law of God, the law of nature, or the law of the ages. These systems of judgment applied to him just as equally as they applied to all other people. They were unalterable and inescapable. As a result, they served to acclimate the European consciousness to thinking of the law as something that is *there*—a real and tangible entity—something more than simply the sum of demands of the most powerful elements in society. As long as law is understood in the latter terms, it will be perceived as illegitimate and will be disregarded. For the rule of law to function, there must be widespread belief that the law is legitimate and that it applies to everyone.

The social constructs described above incubated the rule of law during its nascence in Europe. Unfortunately, these constructs are not present in contemporary China. The dawn of the postmodern age and the horrors of World War II brought an end to the credibility of natural law. To the extent that the Chinese classics can be likened to a religion, the experiences of the nineteenth century and thereafter obliterated belief in divine law. Any meager vestiges of belief that managed to survive were ultimately eliminated by the stranglehold of Marxist dogma. As for customary law, the nominal purpose of the Cultural Revolution was to eliminate the burdensome yoke of tradition. This goal was achieved at the expense of the customary law upon which China relied so heavily for functioning. In Mao's wake, China was left with no customary law, no divine law, no natural law, and no reason to believe that law was anything more than a framework for satisfying the demands of the powerful. In fact, Marxism says that law is just that. Marx referred to law as an instrument of class domination: a way for the wealthy to subdue the poor.[95] Thus, none of the factors which made Europe predisposed to the rule of law were operative in modern China. Although this insight is discouraging, a closer examination of how the rule of law developed in Europe may provide some cause for optimism.

The economic and political systems of feudal Europe were organized hierarchically, with each tier of society owing reciprocal obligations.[96] The serfs owed labor to their feudal lords, who in turn owed food and shelter to their serfs. The feudal lords drew their wealth from landholdings, but their landholdings were contingent upon the favor of the king. The feudal lords owed taxes and military support to the king, who in turn owed protection from foreign aggression and continued land rights to the feudal lords. This system functioned statically for hundreds of years. Every man in his place, and a place for every man—except the merchants. Merchants, an obscure and unorganized group, existed outside of the feudal order. Professor Tamanaha has explained that merchants were free of any of the obligations that bound the serfs, lords, and king, but on the other hand, nobody was obligated to provide the merchants with anything. They had to provide for themselves, and they had to do so without any power in the feudal system. In order to survive under these conditions, the merchants had to optimize their dealings. This prompted the widespread use of contracts, an intelligent system of rights, and rational procedures of proof. The official courts of the land, however, were dominated by the nobility, who continued to apply obsolete and irrational laws and procedures which served to benefit the nobility but often stifled commerce. The church condemned commerce due to the Catholic prohibition against the lending and borrowing of money. In addition to being a religious authority, the medieval church was also a major political force whose bishops owned large tracts of land and wielded accompanying legal power. Thus, there were several prominent forces allied against the merchants.

But there were also prominent forces allied with the merchants. Before the king could wage war, he would first need to raise an army, which required an enormous sum of money. In principle, he was supposed to call upon the feudal lords to support his army with taxes and manpower, but the feudal lords were often reluctant.[97] Part of this reluctance came from concern for the lords' own fortunes—a dollar spent on the war was a dollar that could have been spent on the estate—but another part came from jealousy. Some of the lords schemed to usurp the throne, and building the king's armies did not advance those schemes. Either way, the king was forced to seek funds from extraordinary sources.

On this basis, a marriage of convenience was born between the king and the merchants, whose livelihoods depended on saving and accumulation.[98] The more the merchants prospered, the greater the piggy bank the king could dip into when the nobles were unforthcoming. Thus, the king acquired an interest in facilitating the activities of merchants. One of the merchants' greatest needs was cheap labor. This labor could only be found by siphoning off serfs from the feudal lords. The merchants' other chief imperative was to be unencumbered by the irrational legal conventions perpetuated by the nobles. "Monarchs supported the attempts of the cities, led by the merchants, against the opposition of the nobles, to become self-governing corporations or franchises."[99] These franchises recognized the conventions that the merchants had long used in their private dealings as legally binding, doing away with the conventions of the nobles. Furthermore, any serf who resided in the city for one year was granted freedom.

Of course, the aforementioned alliances were not set in stone. From time to time, the king would ally with the nobles out of a shared sense of jealousy at the merchants' growing prosperity. A particularly bellicose king might attempt to overdraw from the merchants, or a particularly aggressive king might violate the rights of a feudal lord. Under these circumstances, the merchants would ally with the nobles against the king. When the king was accused of misdeeds, he would swear his allegiance to the law. Similarly, whenever a new king ascended to the throne, he would promise to accept the yoke of the law. He would pronounce the law to be the true ruler of the kingdom, and he its mere steward. Almost invariably, this was untrue, but the king understood that it was in his interest to be perceived as such.

Alliances shifted back and forth. War, plague, drought, and famine ravaged the population and disturbed the order. Old kings died and new kings succeeded. The process went on, continuously eating away at the feudal structure. As commerce increased, the wealth of merchants grew large relative to the wealth of the nobles, whose income was dependent on a fixed plot of land. As inflation reduced the wealth of the nobles, they struggled to continue to support their obligations to the serfs and to the king. Land-rich and money-poor, the nobles were gradually forced to sell off their land and sell freedom to their serfs. While this solved their problems temporarily, it undermined the basis of their position in society.

Alliances rocked back and forth. New kings swore by the rule of law. The serfs struggled their way to the cities. The church condemned the king; the king condemned the church. The merchants moved into the estates formerly owned by nobles. The nobles derided the merchants as nouveau riche peddlers of low birth. Alliances shifted again.

Whereas the growth of agriculture is limited by the supply of land and the growth of tax revenue is limited by public consent, the growth of commerce is limited only by human imagination. As a result, each moment that passed brought the merchants greater wealth relative to the nobles and the king. Every time the nobles and the king sold their land in order to keep pace with the merchants, it further undermined their source of power. Due to the constant shifting of alliances, no one group was able to retain any unearned advantages over the others. Any advantages that a group hoped to enjoy had to be justifiable to the other groups. As the merchant class gained a more prominent place in this mix, the rational legal conventions upon which they relied became more important to society at large. Thus, the legal profession prospered.

Professor Tamanaha concludes his explanation "by proposing…*the* essential ingredient to establishing the rule of law, however it is understood. Pervasive societal attitudes about fidelity to the rule of law…[are] the mysterious quality that makes the rule of law work."[100] After generations of being told that the kingdom was ruled by law and that the king, too, was subject to the law, the public came to believe these promises as a matter of fact, and expected their fulfillment.

Nominally, the feudal system remained in place well into the eighteenth century. In practice, however, the most powerful actors in society were the Rothschilds, the Medicis, and other wealthy merchant families. The feudal lords remained powerful in name only, their estates long since scattered. The titles they retained gave them special privileges that would forever be unavailable to the merchants. Wars between kings exacted an ever-greater price on society. The group that bore the brunt of this was the serfs, who met quick death as cannon fodder. These people were taxed to the gills and worked to the brink of collapse, and beyond. As the burden of the common man grew so heavy that he verged on expiration, the people finally rose up and battled the last remaining vestiges of the feudal system. The human will to survive is inspirationally

The Rule of Law

powerful. A man can only be worked so hard and starved for so long before he realizes that he has nothing to lose but his chains. Covered in the ash of his affliction, he will stand upright and throw off the yoke of bondage. This is how the feudal order in Europe finally expired, giving rise to the rule of law.

This account, while neither complete nor detailed, conveys the broad trends of history.[101] Surprisingly, these historical trends find stunning parallels in contemporary China. In an analogy between modern China and feudal Europe, official status, or *guan* (官), in modern China is the proper analogue to landholdings in feudal Europe. Just as the nobles in feudal Europe were marked and empowered by their landholdings, so, too, party cadres in modern China are marked and empowered by their official status. Just as the monarch in feudal Europe was distinguished by the relative size of his landholdings, his power to call upon the other nobles for military service and taxes, and his special status as the nobleman who handled affairs with other kingdoms, so, too, the top leadership of the Communist Party is distinguished from other party cadres by the relative weight of its official status, its ability to call upon other cadres for military service and taxes, and its special status as the representative of China to the outside world. The proper analogues for the religious authorities in feudal Europe are the Communist ideologues in modern China, who similarly disdain commercial enterprise. And, of course, the rising merchant class in feudal Europe is a perfect analogue to the rapidly rising merchant class in modern China. It is a well-documented phenomenon that as the wealth of the merchant class grows large relative to the fixed government salaries of the party cadres and the senior leadership, the latter two groups often attempt to sell the influence of their *guan* in exchange for money. This solves the temporary problem of cash flow but undermines their long-term position. This analogy is applicable right down to the thorny issue of residency in urban cities for serfs from the countryside.

The important thing to emphasize is that China is changing very rapidly. Equality of the masses has long been a dominant theme in Chinese history. There is a phrase in Chinese, *lao bai xing* (老百姓), which literally means "old hundred surnames." In popular use, the phrase means "all people" and is commonly heard in collective descriptions of the masses, such as *lao bai xing* does this or that, and *lao bai xing* feels a certain way about a particular issue. That the phrase is still so commonly used to suggest unanimity and equality amongst the people is an interesting artifact of Chinese sociology. For most of history, most citizens of China, with the exception of the imperial court, lived essentially equivalent lives of hardship and poverty. Thus, for most of Chinese history, it was sensible to paint the citizenry with such a broad brush. But this is no longer the case today. Although *lao bai xing* remains commonplace in popular discourse, enormous diversity exists in Chinese society today, and the diversity is growing by the day. There are high-ranked and low-ranked government officials within the party, and there are prominent people outside of the party. There is a raging sexual revolution sweeping the youth, a growing counterculture, and rising reactionaries.[102]

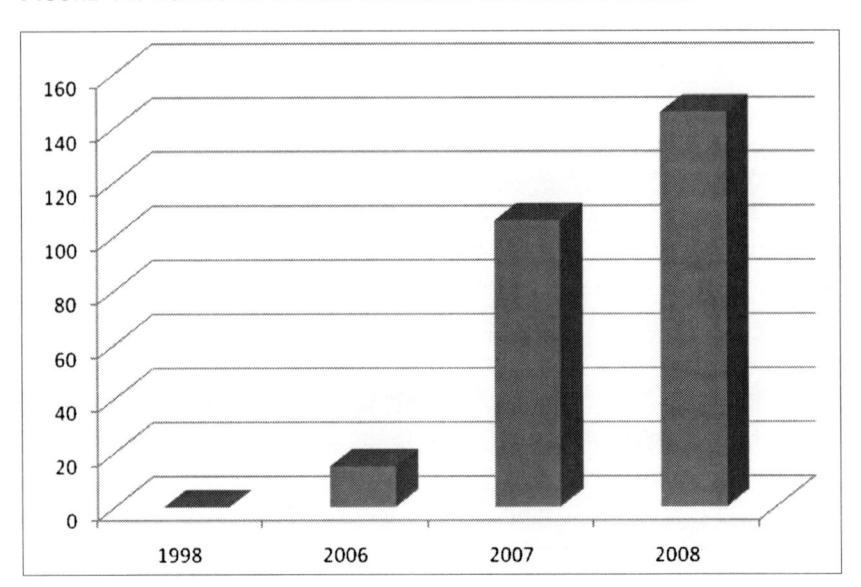

FIGURE 11. Number of Chinese billionaires as a function of time.

Source. Adapted from Cheng (2007) and *China Daily* (2008).

A new class of uberwealthy Chinese has sprung up practically overnight. The number of Chinese billionaires has multiplied tenfold in the last two years alone, currently standing at 146.[103] For example, the latest trend in high-end real-estate development in China is to build luxury communities with names like Orange County, SoHo, Central Park, and Long Beach. Orange County, Beijing, is a $60 million development with 143 units, all of which sold within a month of listing.[104]

At the same time, there are 300 million people living at or below the poverty line of $1 per day.[105] Earlier this year, a Chinese billionaire spent $500,000 for twenty-seven bottles of wine,[106] while there are throngs of people who go to bed hungry each night. There are people with a fervently nationalist perspective, and there are people with an amazingly cosmopolitan perspective. There are people in the countryside who have never traveled more than ten miles from their ancestral homes and wear nothing but rags, and there are people in Shanghai who attended Oxford and wear nothing but designer clothing. The lives, attitudes, and perspectives of each of these groups of people are thoroughly different. It no longer makes sense to describe everyone with one broad brush.

Diversity of opinions, perspectives, and lifestyles is growing at an unbelievable pace. These elements are beginning to coalesce around interest groups. The fortunes of the 146 billionaires create considerable interests to defend. Those 146 people are pursuing a very different agenda from the rest of society and are willing to spend big money to buy influence. On the other hand, provincial governors in the poorest provinces have an interest in some amount of redistribution of wealth, if for no other reason than to keep the peasants from restlessness. Media executives chafe under a system of censorship that stifles competition with foreign firms and plays favorites with domestic firms. The business of lobbying the government is quickly growing into an enormous industry.[107] As interest groups seek champions in the party, we can expect competition within the party to heat up.[108] Alliances will give rise to coalitions, and coalitions will fall as alliances shift. As long as the party is dominated by a particular coalition, the government will draft nonspecific legislation, because the coalition can avail itself of other means to influence interpreters toward a particular interpretation. But if dominance of the party is in contest, then whichever coalition enjoys greater power at the moment will make sure that all legislation produced under its auspices is drafted with specific language in order to constrain future interpretations which may occur under the auspices of a hostile coalition. As prosperity rises and the average Zhou Shmoe has more to defend, he will devote an increasingly greater share of his resources to fighting for his interests. Intraparty competition will heat up, the turnover rate of coalitional dominance will increase, and legislation will, in general, become more specific, as has happened elsewhere.

The economic substructure of China has already undergone profound change and continues to change at a mind-boggling pace. Corresponding change to the political superstructure is always slow in coming, but is inevitable. In the meantime, the exact form of the Chinese state should be viewed as less important than its behavior. Deng Xiaoping said it best: "It doesn't matter if it's a black cat or a white cat, as long as it catches mice."[109] A process has been set in motion that will lead to formal legality, and likely the rule of law, as long as the party does not succumb to the temptation to respond to change with hostility. Indeed, the party seems to be embracing change, even if only in rhetoric. Only a few years ago, the word *democracy* was taboo in Beijing. Today, the concept of intraparty democracy has become the principal platform of President Hu Jintao. On October 15, 2007, Hu delivered the paramount address of his administration to the Seventeenth Party Congress in Beijing. He mentioned democracy sixty times, more than any other political concept.[110] Although Western analysts are inclined to dismiss this as empty rhetoric, some authoritative voices stress that it is a genuine indicator of future policy directions.[111] Whether it is a genuine indicator or empty rhetoric may not matter as much as the fact that it is being officially articulated. As recently as 1997, the Chinese government refused to use the phrase *rule of law* in any official capacity.[112] There was a serious internal debate about whether or not it was acceptable, or wise, to subordinate the party to law, even if only in rhetoric. Alternative phrasing was considered, such as *rule by law* and *ruling the country according to law*.[113] Since that time, the phrase has received the enthusiastic approval of the party. In 1999 the constitution was amended to reflect the desirability of the rule of law.[114] Almost every official communication now contains some reference to the rule of law, and the government has published white papers extolling the great lengths to which it has gone to establish the rule of law.[115]

As stated earlier, "pervasive societal attitudes about fidelity to the rule of law…[are] the mysterious quality that makes the rule of law work."[116] In feudal Europe, this began with opportunistic monarchs making promises about their fidelity to the rule of law, even when they were pathological violators of the law. After generations of hearing that the kingdom was ruled by law, and that the monarch, too, was subject to the law, people came to believe these pronouncements as a matter of fact and demand their fulfillment. So it is with modern China. Just as feudal European monarchs concluded that it was in their best interest to convince the public that the kingdom was ruled by law, so, too, the Chinese government has concluded that it is in its best interest to convince the public that the Middle Kingdom is ruled by law. If these pronouncements are repeated across time, perhaps the Chinese people will come to believe them as a matter of fact and demand their fulfillment.

Conclusion

This chapter began with a definition of the rule of law and proceeded to flesh out the current weaknesses of the rule-of-law system in China. A depiction was then offered of the highly nuanced relationship between the rule of law and the role of lawyers. This relationship explains the role, size, and conditions of the bar as functions of the wording of legislation, the political context in which legislation is drafted, and the economic environment in which politics is transacted. It is a fair characterization to say that this is the whole of China, this is everything that is happening. From this perspective, it is understood that the fate of lawyers is the ultimate bellwether for the Chinese civilization. To this bellwether we cast our gaze in order to grasp at the present and glimpse at the future.

Chapter 4

Becoming a Chinese Lawyer

There is an exciting aura of newness surrounding the legal profession in China. The entire profession is only thirty years old! There is no such thing as a stuffy old law firm or an aged and entrenched partner. Every law firm, law school, partner, professor, course, textbook, and so on, has no more than thirty years of history. To understand the aura of excitement that surrounds the legal profession in China, one must think of the excitement that surrounds Internet start-ups or venture capital in America. There are no established rules or even established rule-makers. The whole field is open, just waiting for gunners to come in and carve out their territory. To young people evaluating their interest in a legal career, these features of newness and openness are incredibly attractive. But it is precisely these features that limit the availability of the type of information that young people typically use to evaluate their interest in a career. In the West, information about legal careers permeates society because the profession is so well established. But in China, information about legal careers is much less accessible. This has something of a negative effect on the ability of young people to make informed decisions about their desired career.

It should be noted that the process of making such decisions in China is very different from the process in America. In the American education system, at the end of high school, students take a standardized test for college admissions and then apply to university. They are encouraged to declare a major on their application forms, but it is not required, and it is not binding. American college students can switch majors as many times as they wish. Thus, they have the privilege of leisurely discovering themselves and figuring out what they want to do with their lives. This is not the case in China. In the Chinese education system, high school students take a standardized test for college admissions and then apply to a specific department within a university. They are required to declare a major on their application form, and the declaration is strictly binding. Thus, they are forced to decide how they wish to spend their lives at a very young age. Making such a consequential decision at such a young age is difficult in any case. But for students considering a career in law, the limited availability of information is a tremendous drawback. Many Chinese lawyers interviewed for this book admitted that their decision to become a lawyer was based principally on what they had learned about lawyers by watching *Boston Legal*, *Ally McBeal*, *Law and Order*, and movies from Hong Kong. One lawyer from Shanghai commented, "When I was in high school, I had no idea what a lawyer actually does. I just knew, from *Ally McBeal*, that lawyers live interesting lives."[1] As time progresses, however, the profession is becoming more established and the information gaps are filling in.

Correspondingly, China is in the middle of a generational drift in popular wisdom regarding career choices for young people.[2] In the 1970s, popular wisdom held that if you studied math or science, you would be set for life. Consequently, the lion's share of Chinese students in the 1970s enrolled in math and science programs. The trend in the 1980s held that if you studied computers or engineering, you would be set for life. As a result, tides of Chinese students poured into technical programs. In the 1990s, it was widely believed that if you studied international topics (international relations, international economics, international finance, international marketing), you would be set for life, so there arose a great wave of students whose degrees began with the word *international*. Popular wisdom in the first decade of the twenty-first century holds that if you study law, you will be set for life. Thus, at the present time, there are hordes of students beating down the gates of law schools in pursuit of a legal education.

What do these students cite as their motivation for wanting to become lawyers? This question could be asked of law students in any country, and one could reasonably expect to hear similar answers. These answers are present in China as well. But beyond the standard answers that one would expect, there are also answers that are very particular to China's developmental, political, and historical experience. The answers generally revolve around three themes: money, independence, and patriotism. Each of these themes will be discussed in turn. Many young Chinese want to become lawyers because they perceive lawyers to be very wealthy.[3] Particularly for young Chinese who come from impoverished provinces, the prospect of becoming a lawyer is seen as an opportunity to catapult in a single generation to a level of prosperity that was never before imaginable. Even if the legal profession does not guarantee great wealth, the average lawyer's income and standard of living is remarkably higher than the national average.

Other young Chinese want to become lawyers because they perceive lawyers to be highly independent.[4] Compared to government-owned corporations, socialized work units, and public utilities, the life of a lawyer is indeed highly independent. It is very common for lawyers in China to find their own clients, set their own hours, and dictate their own billing rates. All that is required to establish a new law firm is three full-time lawyers. There are seemingly limitless opportunities to carve out a career where, when, and how the individual desires. For young people who place a premium on independence, this is very attractive.

Finally, many young people want to become lawyers out of a sense of patriotism.[5] In order to continue China's economic development, to say nothing of political development, justice, and safety, China needs many more lawyers. There is a growing sense among young people that this need is becoming urgent, and that filling this need is the patriotic calling of their generation. One Chinese lawyer who was interviewed for this book said that his inspiration for becoming a lawyer originated in America:

> When I learned about American history in school, I found out that Abraham Lincoln was a lawyer. Then I looked at the other American presidents, and saw that they were all lawyers. This made me think that I should be a lawyer too. China needs a Lincoln.[6]

One lawyer from Jilin described her experience when, as an LLM student at an American law school, she went down to New Orleans with a national group of law students to help victims of Hurricane Katrina:

> The local government was going to pass a law that would be very harmful to the victims. We went to New Orleans to help prevent this. We interviewed residents and were going to meet with the mayor of New Orleans, but the appointment was canceled. This left a very deep impression on me, because I think that is the difference between America and China. In the United States, a lot of people care about issues even when the issues have no impact on them, and they think they can change things, so they do. But in China, most of the people only think about their personal business, nothing else, and they think they can't change *anything*. There were nearly four hundred students who went to New Orleans for this program. So I think that those people believe that they can change the law. They're only students in law school, but they have the idea that they can change the law. I think the law is our power, so we should be able to change it to make it better. But in China, we only read the law book, think about what it says, and how we can apply the law. As lawyers, we should be thinking how can we push the law, how can we change the law, not only remember the book's contents.[7]

There is, in fact, a vanguard of Chinese lawyers that fits this profile. These lawyers push the law and sculpt the law by doing pro bono work on sensitive, high-profile cases. A very prominent lawyer from Shanghai explained his involvement in such cases by alluding to one of the most well-known authors in modern Chinese literature:

> Have you read Lu Xun? He was the father of modern Chinese literature. He wrote a collection of short stories that criticized imperial society. One of the running themes in his work is the idea that social cohesion is absent in Chinese society—everybody's out for number one. Lu Xun's best illustration of this problem is found in his short story "Medicine," which is an account of how the Qing Dynasty would execute revolutionaries who had martyred themselves for social reform. At the time, there was an outbreak of tuberculosis. There was also a prevalent superstition that tuberculosis could be cured by dipping a bun in the blood of a martyr and eating it. Countless people visited the gallows to act on this superstition. What Lu Xun was saying is that the people were extremely selfish. They were blind to the sacrifices that were being made for them. It was a man-eat-man society, both literally and figuratively. China today is still man-eat-man. There are a lot of lawyers that want to help society, but they don't want to become bloody buns.[8]

A lawyer from Guangzhou phrased the issue in a profound way:

> Supreme Court Justice William Rehnquist once said that lawyers are somewhere between businessmen and clergymen. The former are motivated by personal profit without regard to ideals, while the latter are motivated by ideals without regard to profit. The motivation of lawyers is a conflicted mix between personal profit and public profit. How should lawyers find the right balance between the two? This is the question that each lawyer must answer for himself.[9]

The motivations that attract young Chinese people to the legal profession—money, independence, and patriotism—are not mutually exclusive. Some students cite all three as factors which motivated their interest in law.

Several law schools were visited during the research for this book, including People's University in Beijing and Fudan University in Shanghai. People's University and Fudan University are taken to be representatives of the top echelon of legal education. The top ten schools, according to the most recent rankings, are shown in the table below.[10]

One cannot understand the whole field of legal education by visiting only top-tier programs. Needless to say, one would not visit Harvard and Yale to gain an understanding of the average American law school. Although Harvard and Yale are representative of the best, most of America's legal education takes place outside of their hallowed halls. Most of American legal education takes place in very average schools. However, it is not practical to investigate every average school in China. We can nonetheless derive a great deal of understanding of the average school by examining the top-tier schools. Whatever advantages are advertised by the top-tier schools, one would certainly expect to be the envy and

FIGURE 12. Top ten law schools in China.

Rank	Name	Location
1	Beijing University	Beijing
2	People's University	Beijing
3	Wuhan University	Wuhan
4	Qinghua University	Beijing
5	Chinese University of Politics and Law	Beijing
6	Jilin University	Changchun
7	Fudan University	Shanghai
8	Southwestern University of Politics and Law	Chongqing
9	Zhongnan University of Economics and Law	Wuhan
10	Zhejiang University	Hangzhou

Source. Adapted from Sina (2007).

ambition of the average schools. And whatever limitations or shortcomings are found in the top-tier schools one would certainly expect to be present and more pronounced in the average schools. In other words, a visit to a top-tier law school does provide some understanding of the general direction in which the field of legal education is moving, even if most of the schools are not yet in motion. With these thoughts in mind, the following is a collection of insights that we gleaned from visits to People's University and Fudan University and from interviews with administrators of these schools.

A visitor to the law school of People's University would be startled by the modernity and magnificence the school's facilities. The Ming De Building, which houses the law school, the business school, and the journalism school, was completed in 2005. The building itself has a commanding aura of power, and all of its facilities are state of the art. This facility, in fact, puts the facilities of many American law schools to shame. Walking down the hallways of the law school, one notices many inspirational paintings hung on the walls. Each of the paintings depicts a great image from the history of justice. There is a painting of King Solomon adjudicating between two women, both of whom claimed to be the mother of the same child. There is a painting of Roman senators debating in the Forum. There is a painting of British nobles arguing before a court. There is a painting of the signing of the Declaration of Independence. As one advances through the halls, it becomes evident that the great preponderance of the paintings depict Western images of justice. Out of a total of about a dozen paintings, only three feature Chinese images. Those three images are portraits of legal philosophers from around the time of Confucius. One cannot help but wonder, why are there so few Chinese images of justice on display in China's number-two law school? Is it possible that there aren't any other examples or symbols of justice in Chinese history? Could it be that, fundamentally, the leadership of the school conceives of law and lawyers as concepts that are inextricably bound up with Western culture? Whatever the answers are, the dominance of Western images in this setting should certainly make us pause to wonder.

FIGURE 13. *The Declaration of Independence* at People's University Law School.

Source. Original photograph.

We visited Fudan University on multiple occasions. On every occasion, there was a small group of merchants stationed right in front of the law school selling pirated DVDs, music, and books. It seemed highly ironic that they would deign to violate intellectual property rights directly in front of the classrooms in which intellectual property law is taught. This experience demonstrated, in a very powerful way, the fact that certain rights that exist in the classroom have not become a reality on the street, even when the street is adjacent to the classroom.

The facilities of Fudan's law school, unlike those of People's law school, were quite shoddy. There was no air-conditioning, the floors were composed of unfinished concrete, and the desks and chairs resembled something you would expect from the nineteenth century. This is not meant as

FIGURE 14. *Judgment of Solomon* at People's University Law School.

Source. Original photograph.

FIGURE 15. *Papinionous* at People's University Law School.

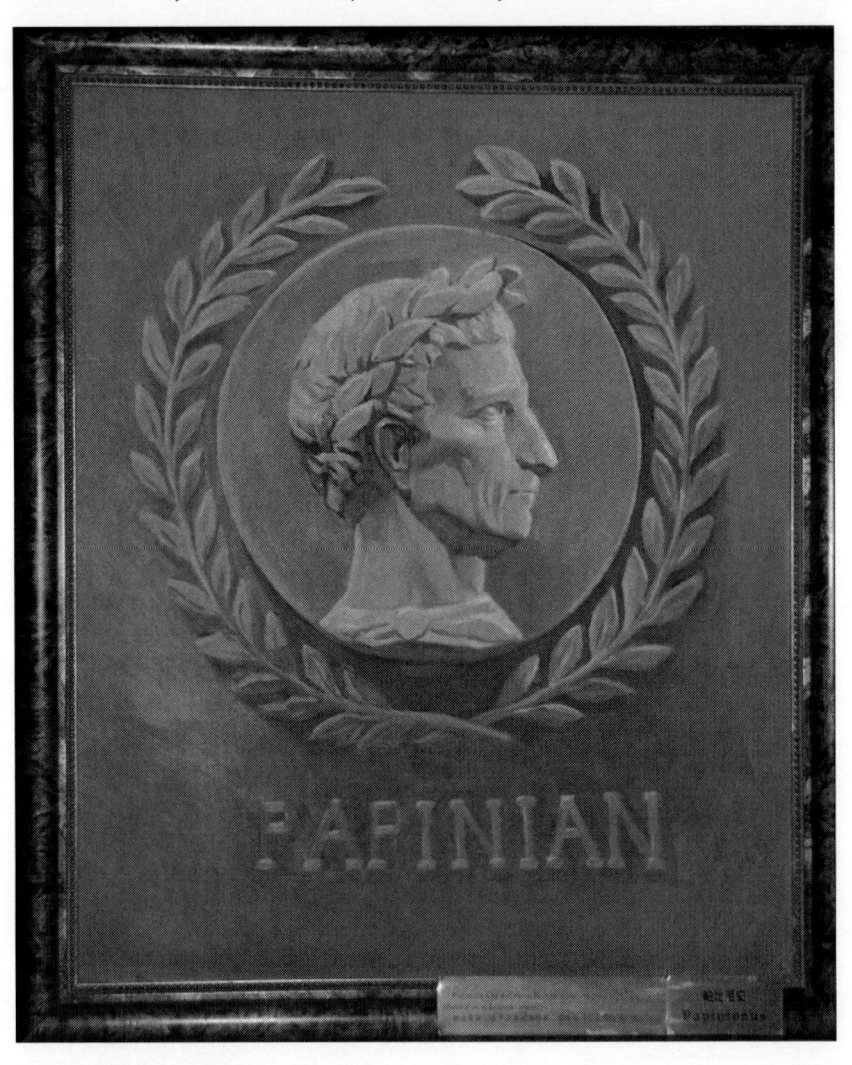

Source. Original photograph.

a knock to Fudan. After all, Fudan is a top-tier school. It is for this reason that we find the low grade of facilities so significant. If a top-tier law school in China's wealthiest city has such poor facilities, how dilapidated must be the lesser schools in poorer provinces? Departmental administrators informed us that the law school was in the process of building a new facility. They bragged that their new facility would trump the facilities of People's University. Thus, it seems as though Chinese law schools are at the beginning stage of a great wave of physical enhancement that will hopefully cascade from the top-tier schools down to the lesser schools.

The undergraduate law curriculum is four years long. Tuition is paid privately and is on the order of $1,000 to $5,000 per academic year.[11] Scholarships and student loans are both available. Although currently, neither form of student aid is as prevalent in China as in the West, they are becoming more popular and more available each year.[12]

There are roughly two hundred universities in China that grant bachelor's degrees in law. (For a full list of these universities, see the appendix.) The number of law schools has exploded in the last ten years in response to surging interest in legal education. The rapid growth of law schools has given rise to concern about the quality of legal education, and rightly so. There are not enough qualified law professors to go around. Many schools do not have adequate peripheral resources such as law libraries and legal-information systems. Some law schools are even lacking in basic infrastructure such as desks and chairs, not to mention wireless Internet. This is not to say that all law schools have such problems, or even the majority. But this set of problems is real, and it affects the whole field. If a substantial number of law schools are churning out undereducated graduates, it affects the baseline of the entire profession. That being said, there are a great number of top-notch law schools in China. Many of the professors in these programs have advanced degrees from prominent institutions in the West and are well published in relevant journals. The enormous demand for legal education has created incredible competition for admission into these programs.

The curricula do not vary substantially from program to program.[13] Nor, for that matter, are the curricula substantially different from their counterparts in the West. Most of the curricular differences between Chinese law schools and Western law schools are explained by the fact of jurisdictional differences, or, in other words, by the fact that the Chinese legal system is simply constituted differently from American and European legal systems. Once this is taken into account, the curricula of Chinese legal education are more or less similar to Western curricula. Chinese lawyers who come to the West to do advanced legal training are the best positioned to assess the differences between the two curricula. They predominately report that the cores of both curricula are very similar.[14] There are required courses in torts, contracts, criminal law, civil procedure, constitutional law, and so on. However, even though the core courses are similar, the supporting coursework and the teaching style are very different. Chinese law schools do not emphasize supporting courses such as legal writing, legal research, or professional ethics. Chinese lawyers who come to the West for advanced training uniformly report amazement at how much of an emphasis Western law schools place on legal writing and research. One female lawyer from Xiamen said, "In China, these are taught, but not enough. And most of the students view them as nothing more than a tool. I don't think it's a tool. I think it's an essential part of being a functional lawyer."[15]

Another prominent difference is teaching style. American law schools use the Socratic method to engage the class in discussion. Chinese law schools rely mainly on lecture-style classes because there are too many students in each class to support a discussion. One lawyer opined, "They lecture at you about legal rules, and you are expected to commit the rules to memory. But you don't engage with the material; you don't think through the reasoning."[16] When we sat in on an undergraduate bankruptcy law class at Fudan University, we counted six students blatantly listening to iPods, nine students reading books unrelated to the lecture, one female student reading the Chinese equivalent of *Cosmopolitan*, and one student peeling an apple with a small knife. To say that those students were not engaged with the material would be a great understatement. Anyone who is familiar with education in China will tell you that this problem is not unique to law schools. Enormous class sizes, rote learning, and emphasis on sterile memorization and regurgitation are features common to all bachelor's-degree programs in China.

Students who continue on to pursue master's degrees and doctoral degrees in law report that the problematic aspects of the teaching style found in undergraduate schools fade away at the postgraduate level.[17] The teaching style in graduate school is more engaging and more geared toward the needs of the individual. The emphasis on memorization and regurgitation of rules is replaced with an emphasis on legal principles, reasoning, argumentation, and abstract thinking. What makes this teaching style practicable at the master's and doctoral levels is that there are far fewer students interested in pursuing advanced degrees than bachelor's degrees, and smaller class size permits interactive discussion and engagement with the material. On the other hand, far fewer students are ever exposed to this sort of training, about which there is a general consensus of superiority.

The anemic demand for graduate education in law is explained by the fact that a graduate degree is not required to sit for the bar exam. Given that students can become lawyers without a graduate degree, many perceive the additional commitment of time required for graduate studies to be unworthy of the sacrificed years of earnings. It may at first strike the reader as surprising that the bar exam does not require a graduate degree in law, but this is the case in most countries. What is truly surprising is that not only does the Chinese bar exam not require a graduate degree in law, it does not even require a bachelor's degree in law. All that is required to sit for the exam is a four-year bachelor's degree in any subject; even a degree in art history will satisfy the requirement.[18] There is an ongoing debate over the wisdom of this policy. Proponents defend it on the basis that it helps the bar to grow by maximizing the number of people who have an opportunity to join the profession. Detractors argue that it inhibits the strength of the bar because it creates a channel for unqualified people to enter the profession, thus dragging down the average level of competency. Although both sides have valid arguments, debating their relative merits is not our current focus. Our current focus is discussing the nature of the bar examination and channels for entry into the legal profession.

The bar exam is held in the middle of September. The exam is currently only offered one time per year, although there are calls to offer it twice per year. The registration fee for the exam is quite reasonable, between two hundred and three hundred renminbi ($30–$40), and the exam is proctored in every major city in the country. The exam is two days long, consisting of four sections. Each section is worth 150 points, for a maximum score of 600 points. Students who score 360 or greater pass the exam and are granted an A-class lawyer's certificate. Students who score 340 or greater pass the exam and are granted a B-class lawyer's certificate. Students who score below 340 do not pass the exam, but remain eligible for registration the following year. The overall passage rate is very low. As such, passing the exam is seen as a tremendous achievement.

An A-class lawyer's certificate confers the right to engage in legal practice nationwide with certain limitations. A B-class lawyer's certificate confers the right to engage in legal practice only in certain less-developed provinces, such as Xinjiang and Tibet, also with certain

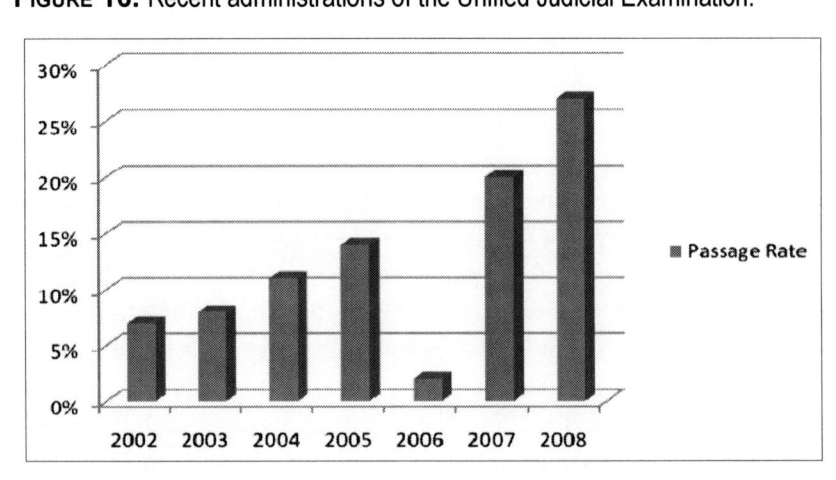

FIGURE 16. Recent administrations of the Unified Judicial Examination.

Source. Adapted from Sina Education, "National Unified Judicial Examination High Passage Rate Opportunity." (2009).

limitations. In order to explain the nature of the limitations, we must first define precisely what it means to be a lawyer.

In order to practice law in the People's Republic of China, one must be a member of the bar association. Every member of the bar association is issued a lawyer's license, which must be renewed annually. Possession of a lawyer's license confers the right to perform the functions of an attorney on behalf of clients in all interactions with the government, such as appearing before a court. If the client's needs do not require interactions with the government, then there is effectively nothing to stop an unlicensed individual from providing legal services in exchange for money and calling himself a lawyer. However, possession of a lawyer's license and membership in the bar are powerful indicators of competence, reliability, and reputation. Thus, although some room exists in which unlicensed lawyers can provide legal services, anyone who wishes to have a career as a lawyer has a strong interest in obtaining a lawyer's license. Individuals who pass the bar exam and receive a lawyer's certificate essentially function as unlicensed lawyers. They can be hired by law firms or for other law-related jobs, and they can perform all the functions of a lawyer except those that involve interaction with the government. After they have been successfully employed in a law-related job for one year, then they will automatically be granted a lawyer's license by the Ministry of Justice. Only if their employment is terminated prematurely or if they demonstrate terrible incompetence would they not be granted a lawyer's license. It is very rare for an individual to obtain the certificate and not obtain the license.

The period of time between receipt of the certificate and receipt of the license should not be seen as some sort of stumbling block or effort to hold young lawyers back. Rather, it should be seen as a probationary period, a mechanism for weeding out those who are truly unfit to function in the legal world. It should also be seen as a rite of passage. Compensation during this probationary period is very low. Thus, only individuals who have a great deal of enthusiasm and a very high estimation of their own potential would be expected to endure the long and hard hours of a junior associate without commensurate compensation.

After a year of grueling work and low compensation, junior associates are finally granted a lawyer's license. With this license, they are able to practice law anywhere in the country. They are able to perform all of the functions of a lawyer without any limitations. If an individual wishes to become a judge, the process is more or less the same up until this point. Judicial aspirants must get a bachelor's degree from a four-year college, pass the bar exam, and work for one year to earn a lawyer's license. For an individual who is interested in the bench, it makes more sense to spend that year working in a court rather than in a law firm. There are a variety of entry-level positions in the courts. For example, one of our interview subjects worked as a clerk in a Shanghai court. Individuals who work in such positions for one year will receive a lawyer's license. After receiving their lawyer's license, they are eligible for elevation to the bench. This process can vary substantially from one court district to another. In developed jurisdictions with a high number of lawyers per capita, competition for judgeships is very intense. In less developed jurisdictions with a low number of lawyers per capita, competition is not as great. Where there is more competition, there is a more formalized and demanding application process; where there is less competition, the process is less formal and less demanding. At a minimum, the process requires submitting an application for employment to the human resources office of the local court. There is a requirement that judicial applicants "have fine political and professional quality and…be good in conduct,"[19] which opens the door to questions about the role of politics and loyalties in hiring decisions, but in principle, each applicant is assessed on the basis of education and work experience. In the end, all decisions regarding human resources are subject to the discretion of the president of the local court, who is appointed by the local people's congress. If an applicant is approved, she will be granted a position as a junior judge. From this point, she can learn and grow into the judiciary, earn promotions, and advance through the ranks of the court system.

The descriptions above are a rough sketch of the channel for entering into the legal profession. This channel may seem challenging or problematic, but it is a substantial improvement over the channels of the past. When the legal profession was first revived in 1979, the channels for entry into the profession were confusing and irrational. There were low educational requirements or, in some cases, no educational requirements. People were specially invited to join the bar, judges were fashioned out of generals, and prosecutors were drawn from party rank and file. Since 1979, this irrational and confusing maze of channels has been greatly simplified and streamlined through a gradual process of refinement. Today, there is one unified process for entering the legal profession (including the judiciary). This is incredibly important for the health of the legal profession, for without a rational, unified process for entering the field, the bar cannot undergo sustained growth in size, strength, or maturity.

Chapter 5

A Day in the Life

Several Chinese lawyers interviewed for this book mentioned that their motivations for becoming lawyers were founded on expectations set by the exciting lives depicted by *Ally McBeal* and *Boston Legal*. Although it will strike the reader as no surprise that these expectations are infrequently met, there may be some curiosity as to what life is actually like for Chinese lawyers. What are their daily activities? How do they practice their craft? Last year, a book was published in China called *Dancing through Red Dust*, which seeks to answer these questions by walking the reader through the daily labors and moral struggles of modern Chinese lawyers.[1] Although this book is fictional and at some points dramatized, it does provide something of a vista into the lives of Chinese lawyers. With the same purpose in mind, the following anecdotes were collected from interviews with Chinese lawyers. Each group of anecdotes serves to illustrate one noteworthy feature of life as a lawyer in China.

Mentorship and Networking

A famous maxim holds that it's not about what you know, but who you know. Nowhere is this truer than in China. There is a substantial literature about the role of *guanxi* in business and government,[2] and *guanxi* has occupied an important position in the world of law since the revival of the legal profession in 1979.[3] Near the end of the twentieth century, some commentators began to prognosticate that *guanxi* would decline in significance as formal legal institutions grew more entrenched and powerful, but those predictions have gone largely unfulfilled. The enduring prominence of *guanxi*, and the extent to which the practice of *guanxi* cultivation remains intertwined with nightlife, remain noteworthy features of the Chinese legal world.

Guanxi is important not only for finding clients but also for cultivating relationships with other lawyers. Of the lawyers interviewed for this book, nearly all those under the age of thirty made mention of their "mentor." The ubiquity of these sorts of comments might lead one to believe that mentorship is a formal institution of the Chinese bar association, but in general, it is not. Most young lawyers seek out mentors on an informal basis in order to fill in the gaps left by their law school education and to compensate for the lack of guidance from their supervisors. The following anecdotes from Chinese lawyers illustrate the role of *guanxi* and mentorship in their daily lives.

Anecdote 1[4]

> Today a friend reminded me how important it is to network, especially with an older, more experienced lawyer. I just don't know where to start since I'm new. Probably need some time. To find a mentor is not easy when you're a newcomer. But then again, a seasoned lawyer is also very busy, and for them to find an effective assistant is not so easy as well. Therefore, I was thinking I should just first work effectively, so that I can catch someone's attention and they will want me to be that mentee/assistant.

Anecdote 2[5]

> There is a party tonight. Everyone from the firm is going to have dinner together to get to know each other. I heard there is an informal rule in the firm: if you are a lawyer at this firm, you must know how to drink. The higher your tolerance, the more you like alcohol, the better. [*Laughs*], good thing I'm not afraid to drink.

Anecdote 3[6]

> When I first graduated law school, I really didn't know anything about practicing law. The classes don't teach you what lawyers actually do, they just teach you to memorize some sections of the code. When I first started working, my boss expected me to know how to write a legal document, where to go to file a document with the court, et cetera. But I had no idea! That's why you have to seek out a mentor. If you get a really good mentor, he can show you how to practice law. Otherwise, what can you do?

Anecdote 4[7]

> If you really want to get ahead, you have to take judges out to dinner, maybe take them out for drinks. If you don't do that, there's no way for you to get to know the judges. Plus, judges expect it, so if you didn't take them out and you find yourself in court against another lawyer that has a reputation for taking judges out, then the judge might have a grudge against you.

Anecdote 5[8]

> How do I get clients? I think it's probably the same as how American lawyers get clients. I talk to my friends, family, classmates, neighbors. I talk to everyone I know. Beyond that, you do anything you can do to promote yourself to the public. I host a radio talk show where people can call in and ask about their legal problems.

> I give them advice for free, but this does a good job of letting people know who I am, and what my name is, and that I give good advice. I have friends who try to achieve the same thing by teaching courses. Also, it is very helpful if you have experience working for the government, because then you are familiar with how that department works, and you know the people there. If you know the people, it is easier to get hired for jobs.

STRUGGLE

Due to the oversupply of new law graduates, the job market for Chinese lawyers is extremely competitive. Even jobs that are relatively poorly compensated are highly contested. Under such circumstances, the negotiating posture of each individual lawyer is very weak. For most lawyers, the only way they can distinguish themselves to employers is by working harder, longer, and for less money than their colleagues. This is particularly true for graduates of second- and third-tier law schools, against whom there is a popular presumption of inferior capability; in order to overcome that presumption and its attendant stigma, they have to work extra hard. These topics are taken up in depth in chapter 7, "The Market for Chinese Lawyers."

Anecdote 6[9]

> Yesterday, we had a conference that lasted the entire afternoon, until probably 6 p.m. One of the partners then proposed to take us all out to eat. We went to this great restaurant that specializes in preparing fish in every way imaginable. They cook fish in scallion sauces, ginger sauces, soy sauces. They fry, steam, and smoke the fish, and then use the other parts to make fish balls. I had a really good time but the mao-tai liquor made me sick. I went home around 10:00 p.m., showered, and crashed.

Anecdote 7[10]

> Today around noon, this senior associate wanted to come to eat lunch with us. We had a feeling that it was going to be "lecture

time." Turns out we were right. He told us that we must work really hard if we want to grow as lawyers. If we want to succeed, we must give more time and energy than the person next to us. This motivated me but also made me feel ashamed of myself. It was very difficult to land a job this good without *guanxi*. Overall, the firm atmosphere is collegial. No one stands in the way of our growth. This makes me want to take on more responsibilities. I always say I work hard, but let's be real. I waste a lot of time. On weekends, I just watch *Prison Break* and other American miniseries. I don't use that time to learn the law, review the law.

I need to make my weekends more productive from now on. It will give me a great head start. I wanted to use the weekend to date but there is no suitable person right now. If someone catches my eye, then we'll talk.

Anecdote 8[11]

I ride the subway to work every day. Isn't the Shanghai subway nice? I am not from the city, so I always watch in amazement as these well-dressed metropolitans rush in and out of the subway every morning and every night. It makes me proud to be a member of the posh, "white-collar" crowd. We all just get on and off of the subway in one crowded pack. That's life, I guess.

Anecdote 9[12]

When we want to hire a new lawyer, and we're looking at resumes, we either want a student from a top school, or a top student from a mediocre school. The first preference is immediately understandable, but the second might not be. The graduates of second- and third-tier schools from the countryside have a chip on their shoulders. If they are lucky enough to get a job at a firm in the city, they feel like they have to prove themselves. They come here, and they work extra hard to try to show that they're good enough. They'll work through the night if you ask them to. In a sense, they're even more desirable than the graduate [*sic*] of the top schools, because those kids have a sense of entitlement.

Lack of Specialization

It is very uncommon for a Chinese lawyer to specialize in any particular area of law. Most practitioners are generalists. This is explained, in part, by a dearth of work. A lawyer can only afford to specialize if there is enough demand for a particular type of service. For most practice areas in China, the demand is insufficiently robust to justify specialization. The lack of specialization is also explained by the structure of Chinese law firms, which are not designed around a system of apprenticeship. In general, partners train associates to be assistants rather than colleagues. The widespread practice of mentorship, described above, is viewed as the associate's solution to the lack of training by partners. This topic will be discussed in depth in chapter 7, "The Market for Chinese Lawyers." For now, suffice it to say that the absence of apprenticeship is not conducive to specialization.

Anecdote 10[13]

> My trial schedule is always jam-packed. This afternoon, I have to appear at the Hong Kou Trial Court to argue a corruption case. The day after tomorrow, I have to appear at the Second Intermediate Court to argue an injury case. A week after that, I will be trying an illegal drug trafficking case before the Second Intermediate Court. Amidst all of this, I am waiting for the court to set a date for the securities fraud case I just got retained for.

Anecdote 11[14]

> If you're a lawyer, people think you are competent to do things that are not even truly legal in nature. An acquaintance of mine invited me to attend his wedding. When I showed up, he told me, "Because you're here, the wedding is valid." He was not joking. "What do you mean?" I asked. He explained that it was his understanding that my status as a lawyer qualified me to act as a justice of the peace, and therefore, to officiate his wedding ceremony.

A Day in the Life

Anecdote 12[15]

> In China, it's just not that hard to pick up a new area of law and learn everything you need to know about it. You don't have to familiarize yourself with older cases because it's not a common law system, and although you do have to familiarize yourself with statutes, there are only so many statutes. Unlike your statutes, our statutes are not that long. The goal is to browse the language of the statute and get a general idea of what it says. To "specialize" is to refuse certain kinds of case [*sic*]. Why would anyone do that?

Anecdote 13[16]

> Where is my legal library? What do you mean? You mean statutes, I see. I don't really consult statutes. They say pretty much what you expect them to say. But they're never enforced the way you expect them to be enforced. For every area of law, you pretty much just have to know how the judge works and make that your specialty.

TENSION WITH AUTHORITY

One of the most common themes in any discussion with Chinese lawyers is tension with and suspicion of authority. In some cases, the suspicion is well founded, and in some cases, it is not. Lawyers frequently question the prudence of the actions taken by police, judges, and bureaucrats. The pervasiveness of these questions can, at times, lead one to seriously question the extent to which lawyers assign a sense of legitimacy to the authority of governmental and judicial decision makers.

Anecdote 14[17]

> Two men got into a dispute on the bus, and the driver kicked them off. The older man pulled out a knife. The younger tried and succeeded in taking the knife from the older man. At one point, he

stabbed the older man in the thigh. Unfortunately, the older man lost a lot of blood, and died. When the police arrived, they arrested the younger man and charged him with murder. The police's theory was, when two people get into a fight and one dies, the survivor is guilty of murder. I tried the case at the lower court level. I didn't know the identity of any witnesses, so I posted ads in the *Shanghai Daily Evening* newspaper to prompt witnesses to come forward. Two months passed. No one responded to my advertisement. As a result, the only evidence we had was the defendant's version of the story. We lost the case at the trial court level. Conviction for a crime like this usually results in a sentence of ten years in jail. I decided to appeal. After three rounds of argument in the intermediate court, the prosecutor actually came to agree with us that there is simply no evidence in this case other than the defendant's testimony. The defendant chose not to plead guilty. Nonetheless, the court found the defendant guilty and wrote in the opinion that "although the prosecutor agrees with the defendant, their opinion should not be adopted. The defendant should be treated as if he pled guilty, which reduces his sentence by one year. He shall serve nine years in prison."

If the defendant and prosecutor are in agreement, how can the judge say otherwise?

Anecdote 15[18]

After spring festival, I was still in vacation mode. Shortly after returning to Shanghai, I received a call from a woman. Half-sobbing, she told me that her husband's case was about to go to trial. She saw me on TV and wanted me to represent her husband. I did not want to be disturbed since I was still in spring festival mode. But when she started to cry uncontrollable [*sic*], I felt guilty, so I agreed to meet her.

The story goes like this. Her husband knows medicine pretty well. With cooperation from the local hospital, he built a Web site for patients to communicate to one another about their illnesses, coping strategies, and medical needs. One day, a patient posted a complaint about the price of a certain drug. This prompted many patients to commiserate about the price of this drug. These complaints caught the attention of her husband. He had an affiliation with a pharmaceutical company that enabled him to purchase this drug at wholesale price, which was less than one-third of the retail price. He decided to offer the drug to these patients for much less than the retail price but more than the wholesale price so that he could make a small profit.

Because he never applied for a "drug sales license," the prosecutor charged him with illegal sale of drugs. The husband and wife acknowledged that he broke the law by virtue of selling this drug without a license. They just wanted me to get him a lighter sentence. The statutory punishment for the illegal sale of drugs is six years. An examination of all of the documents showed that the drugs were all authentic, name-brand medication. The drug's manufacturer had proper licenses, and even gave the defendant a blank "sales authorization" document to fill out. The defendant was essentially an "authorized dealer" of the drugs. He just didn't get the proper license and paperwork from the government.

I agreed to represent the husband in court. The case resulted in an unusually lively debate in court. The judge was young, but the extensive training he went through taught him how to keep a poker face that did not reveal any emotions. However, when the defendant mentioned that he wanted to be in his one-year-old daughter's life, he moved a bit and looked away. Three weeks later, the court found for the People and gave the defendant a six-year sentence.

The judge in this case was so stone cold! If China had a jury system, the defendant would have been excused or given a much lighter sentence.

Anecdote 16[19]

When someone has a grievance, he or she can start a petition at their local Bureau for Letters and Calls, or *xin fang jü* (信访局). More often than not, the local bureau either ignores the petitioner or forces them to attend reeducation sessions known as "law study groups." Many of these "law study groups" are set up to harass and abuse petitioners. The bureaus pay off nearby hotels to host these "law study groups." I do a lot of pro bono work in this area. I travel with many similar-minded colleagues to these "black jails" to rescue petitioners from illegal detainment, which could be anywhere from two days to ten days. We go into these "black jails" and ask the police to release detained petitioners. In the event they refuse to do so, we show them copies of China's constitutional law and criminal procedure law, which contain provisions that clearly prohibit illegal detainment. Given that it's in the constitution, it is hard to understand why the police are so reluctant to release them.

Anecdote 17[20]

The Beijing Bar Association's annual elections took place last week. I could not believe that the bar association of Beijing, *the capital of China*, would publicly condone an election that was rigged. I could not believe that the biggest bar association in China would turn a blind eye to preestablished election policies and procedures. Several upstanding lawyers that I know should have appeared on the ballot because they jumped through all of the requisite hoops. Yet, certain individuals, motivated by personal advancement and greed, eliminated their names from the ballot at the last minute. If even the lawyers' association cannot operate transparently, then what can?

Anecdote 18[21]

Some disputes have a political side to it, for example, when the defendant is the government. You are the lawyer. Do you take the case or not? The plaintiff needs your help and representation. But you need to keep your job. Most lawyers are afraid of participating in politically sensitive cases in any manner, including referring these cases to other lawyers. I try to get involved as much as I can. I can get away with more because I have a great reputation in the community. My wife is not happy with this because she feels like I am jeopardizing the family's safety. But someone has to do it, right? I belong to an intimate group of lawyer-activists. Most of us are big-firm lawyers by day, activists by night. When we see these cases, we try to take them ourselves, or, if we're too busy, refer them to another lawyer in the group. We've developed codes for referring cases so that when we do it over the phone or e-mail, our message does not get flagged or filtered.

Conclusion

The forgoing anecdotes illustrate several aspects of daily life as a Chinese lawyer. Over the course of countless hours of candid interviews, several of these aspects began to coalesce into themes, and the themes began to congeal into patterns. The purpose of this chapter was to give three-dimensional, human expression to those patterns. The task of the remaining chapters is to analyze those patterns in order to form an understanding of their significance with respect to the political, historical, and economic context in which they are expressed.

Chapter 6

Frustrations in the Practice of Law

No matter where you are, the life of a lawyer is not easy. The hours are long, the competition is stiff, and the work is simultaneously tedious and demanding. Thus, there is no shortage of reasons for lawyers to feel frustrated. But the problems that particularly frustrate Chinese lawyers are not those that you might expect. We asked dozens of Chinese lawyers which aspect of their profession they liked the least. Although all of the responses were slightly different, they were not too different; several patterns emerged repeatedly. The purpose of this chapter is to give voice to their frustration.

A young female lawyer who works in intellectual property practice at the Shanghai office of a major American law firm jokingly explained that the greatest frustration in her job is that she is "surrounded by fake designer purses and designer clothes all day. My professional responsibility is to prosecute and discourage these knockoffs…but some of them would look really good in my closet. It's a serious conflict of interest."[1]

There is a category of frustration that is particular to young lawyers, those who have recently graduated from school. A chief source of frustration for young lawyers is finding their first job. There are only so many jobs available each year, and those that are available are extremely competitive, just as in the West. The high degree of competition for a limited number of jobs means that the starting salary of lawyers must be very low (this topic will be explored fully in chapter 7, "The Market for Chinese Lawyers").[2] For those graduates who are fortunate enough to get jobs, many are disappointed by their starting salaries, which do not measure up to the expectations that they had formed from movies and television shows.[3] Of course, the only thing more disappointing than a low starting salary is no starting salary or, even worse, a negative starting salary. The growth in demand for lawyers is so low relative to the number of law students that graduate each year that some firms are actually able to convince new graduates to work for free for a year, or to pay the firm for the opportunity to work for a year! As one lawyer lamented, "Sometimes the new lawyers get nothing from their firms, or have to pay them. It's really hard to make it through those first few years."[4] The firms justify these practices by claiming that a new lawyer does more learning on the job than working on the job, so they ought to pay the firm for the opportunity to receive this applied education. Whether or not this claim is valid, the paltry wages that new lawyers are accustomed to receiving is a substantial source of frustration.

Lawyers at all levels are frustrated with information barriers. In this chapter, we shall identify three information barriers. The first information barrier is the difficulty involved in accessing official documents such as public records, legal statutes, judicial opinions, or any other document a lawyer might need in order to undertake his professional duties. In the West, these documents are all available on the Internet through subscription legal-database services such as LexisNexis or Westlaw. Thus, a Western lawyer can access these documents instantaneously from any location in the world. LexisNexis has a site for Chinese law, and there is a domestic competitor called Beida Fabao (北大法宝). However, the subscription fees for both services are so high that almost nobody is willing to subscribe. For example, one of the top five firms in Beijing, Fang Da Partners, does not subscribe to any legal database.[5] There are several free Web sites in China that provide the text of legal statutes, but they are not sufficiently comprehensive for a professional lawyer to rely upon them. The only comprehensive source for official documents is the court. If a lawyer needs to acquire the text of a document, he must physically make a trip to the relevant courthouse. Every time the lawyer wishes to obtain another document, another trip must be made.

Once the lawyer has obtained the legal statute or judicial opinion that he is seeking, it is often difficult to convert these documents into a useful map of the rights and responsibilities that they prescribe. This is the second information barrier: authoritative interpretations of the law are difficult to find or synthesize. Many of the lawyers interviewed for this book attribute this problem to the fact that the law leaves too many issues unaddressed. According to one lawyer from Beijing, the essence of this problem can be traced to the misbegotten hierarchy of Chinese law:

> In principal, law is supposed to be like a pyramid, with the constitution at the top and local regulations and rules at the bottom, and nationwide laws in the middle. In reality in China, it's an upside-down pyramid. The local regulations are the most important, then the nationwide laws, and at the bottom, finally, is the constitution.[6]

The third information barrier is the difficulty of bringing information to bear in a trial; "although Chinese courts have subpoena power, there is no legal penalty for witnesses' failure to comply with a court's subpoena."[7] Without any muscle behind the subpoena, many lawyers find it difficult to bring the testimony of reluctant witnesses to trial. Oftentimes, this prevents lawyers from pursuing the optimal litigation strategy. These three information barriers—difficulty in accessing official documents, difficulty in arriving at authoritative interpretations, and difficulty in obtaining reluctant testimony—are commonly cited by Chinese lawyers as substantial sources of frustration.

Figure 17. Inverted pyramid of mandatory authority in the Chinese legal system.

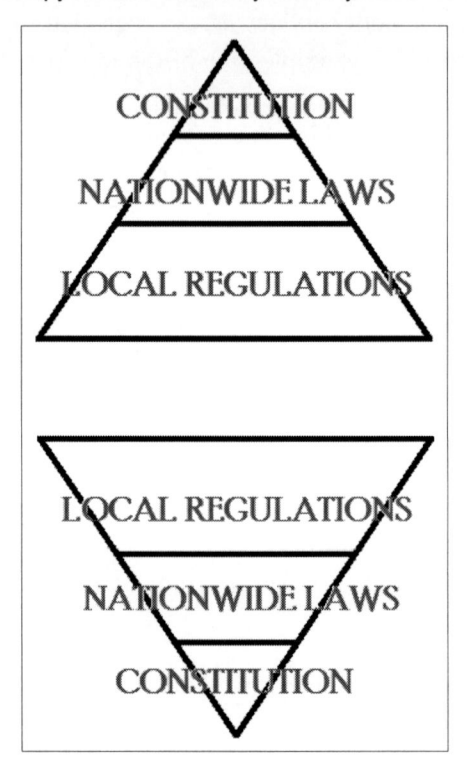

```
         CONSTITUTION
       NATIONWIDE LAWS
      LOCAL REGULATIONS

      LOCAL REGULATIONS
       NATIONWIDE LAWS
         CONSTITUTION
```

Source. Original image.

Another great source of frustration in the lives of Chinese lawyers is the judiciary. *Most* lawyers are of the opinion that the *majority* of judges are unprofessional or corrupt. The caveat to this opinion is that lawyers universally agree that the professionalism and rectitude of the judiciary has clearly improved over the last ten years—but the lawyers remain unsatisfied. A lawyer from Shanghai related to us the following true story:

> I used to work at the court as a clerk. Every day, the judges would go out to lunch together, and they would always come back to work drunk. One day after lunch, a judge came back to work to

officiate a trial, and as soon as he sat down on the bench, he passed out. I nudged him and said, "Judge, you have to start the trial." "Is the plaintiff here?" he mumbled. I said yes. "Is the defendant here?" he mumbled. I said yes. Through his drunken stupor, he slammed his hand on the table and shouted, "Check please!"[8]

Two lawyers from Nanjing claimed that it is rarely possible to escape an interaction with a judge without offering a bribe.[9] Several female lawyers described experiences in which judges demanded sexual favors.[10] Certainly, we are not insinuating that all Chinese judges carry on in this way. But it does appear, based on anecdotal evidence, that the standard of judicial behavior remains quite low. This is a tremendous source of frustration in the lives of Chinese lawyers.

The next source of frustration negatively impacts lawyers, law professors, graduate students, and the entire Chinese academic system itself. In China, the publication and distribution channels of academic journals are centrally organized through the government. Each journal must bear a government-issued serial number, called a *kan hao* (刊号), that uniquely identifies that periodical. If a journal does not bear a *kan hao*, then it may not be published or distributed through the official channels. This, in and of itself, does not constitute a problem. However, the government established a quota for the number of *kan haos* available, and the quota has long since been met. As a result, it is not possible to create any new journals unless an existing journal goes out of business. Over the last twenty years, the number of scholars attempting to publish journal articles has increased substantially as a natural function of the growth of the university system. Today, the number of existing journals is profoundly inadequate to support the number of existing scholars—there simply is not enough space on the pages to publish all, or even most, of the valuable contributions that they create. To complicate matters, the Ministry of Education mandated a nationwide rule that all graduate students at the master's and doctoral levels must publish two articles in scholarly journals before they can receive their degrees.[11] Clearly, this rule is a bit optimistic—not every graduate student is creative enough or motivated enough to come up with two contributions of sufficient novelty and value that would make them worthy of journal publication. This rule, which artificially raises the demand for journal space, combined with the government quota for *kan haos*, which artificially limits the supply of journal space, makes every page of every journal an extraordinarily valuable commodity. This, in turn, places the editor of every journal in a position of considerable power. Given that the career advancement of every professor depends on accumulating publications, these conditions are rife for corruption. Indeed, the practice of bribing journal editors in exchange for publications is quite widespread. In principle, the articles that ought to be published are those that do the most to advance the field of study. If, instead, the articles that are published are those that come with the highest bribe, the field of study will not advance. According to the Vice Dean of the Fudan University Law School, Professor Zhang Guojun, this is one of the most frustrating problems in Chinese law schools and in Chinese universities generally.[12] This dynamic stifles the pace of academic advancement, cheapens the professoriat, and undermines the integrity of the entire education system.

Obviously, this complex of problems has a negative impact on all fields of academia and all of the professions that are premised thereupon. But it has a particularly pronounced impact on the legal profession. Lawyers rely on law journals as a means of analyzing new developments, disseminating new ideas, and uniting the profession. Law journals are the primary mode of communication that transforms lawyers from a disparate group of independent actors into a professional body with specialized knowledge. The dysfunction of this mode of communication lies at the heart of many of the most frustrating problems experienced by the Chinese legal community.

The final source of frustration that this chapter will explore is the role of the lawyer in business. Many Chinese lawyers interviewed for this book were extremely frustrated by the narrow role that businesspeople have carved out for them. One lawyer from Jilin said,

> They only come to lawyers to help settle disputes, never to help prevent disputes. Businessmen should incorporate lawyers fully into the day-to-day aspects of the business, as advisors, to help the business understand the legal consequences of its actions

before they act. If someone acts without thinking about the consequences and then comes to us to fix their problems, we can't do as much to help them.[13]

As an interesting aside, we must note that the practice of billing by the hour is extremely uncommon in China. In fact, the only firms that use the billable-hours arrangement are those that cater to foreign clients. Firms that cater to the domestic market almost exclusively use a prenegotiated fee-for-service arrangement. When asked why billable hours are so uncommon in China, a lawyer from Shanghai responded, "It's a cultural thing. Chinese people are uncomfortable with the idea of agreeing to an open-ended bill, which is inherently difficult to audit or contest. We feel that it places too much trust and power in the other person."[14] Many lawyers in the West would be delighted by his comment. To American lawyers, the principal source of dissatisfaction with their jobs is the billable hour.[15] However, there are two problems with a prenegotiated fee-for-service arrangement. First of all, under that arrangement, the lawyer negotiates his price based on what he thinks the case will involve before he gets his feet wet. In the event of unforeseen circumstances that make the case more demanding than he originally anticipated, the prenegotiated price becomes inadequate. The only way to avoid that eventuality is to refuse to take cases that appear to require an undeterminable level of involvement. Some of the most consequential, landmark trials can drag on for a decade. But under a prenegotiated fee-for-service arrangement, no rational lawyer would accept those cases. Second, even if there are no unforeseen circumstances, a price that is agreed upon in advance for a service that will be delivered in the future provides very little incentive for the lawyer to work hard. Once the price has been determined, the incentives acting on the lawyer are such that he will do the least amount of work necessary to avoid an outcome that would cause the client to begrudge him the fee. This liberates the lawyer to redeploy his time and energy to other cases, where he will perform at a similarly low level. Only by maximizing the number of cases that he accepts can he maximize his revenue. By contrast, the billable-hours arrangement incentivizes the lawyer to maximize the amount of time spent on each case. Critics of billable hours assert that it incentivizes lawyers to spend more time than is really needed. We will not attempt to refute that assertion. However, we will posit that if you were a businessman who was concerned about the legal consequences of your actions, you wouldn't want your lawyer to gloss over even a single detail which might be relevant to the liability of your business. This requires the lawyer to digest every word of every correspondence, brief, statute, public notice, and so on. From that perspective, one would prefer that the lawyer do more work than what is necessary rather than the least amount of work necessary to avoid a confrontation. For this reason, in terms of providing advisory services, the billable-hours arrangement is better suited than the prenegotiated fee-for-service arrangement.[16] By *advisory services*, we mean advising a client on the legal consequences of his day-to-day business operations.

Thus, it appears that the aversion to billable hours that stems from Chinese cultural preference is not compatible with a larger role for lawyers in business. If lawyers are to be incorporated into the process of making business decisions, the billable-hours arrangement must be adopted. This raises the question, are lawyers excluded from the decision-making process because billable hours is not the dominant arrangement, or is billable hours not the dominant arrangement because lawyers are excluded from the decision-making process? We believe that the latter explanation is correct. Our justification for this belief is twofold. First, when cultural tastes come into conflict with the directives of the market, the market tends to win out. If a strong demand for advisory services existed, then cultural preferences regarding billing form would probably be altered as a matter of economic imperative. Second, the exclusion of lawyers from the decision-making process is highly compatible with the notion that Chinese businessmen are not particularly concerned with the legal consequences of their actions. We know that notion to be true from other avenues of our inquiry, such as the discussion of the culture of liability found in chapter 3, "The Rule of Law." In this light, we perceive the dominance of the fee-for-service arrangement as an indicator of a weak culture of liability, and any growth of the billable-hours arrangement is to be perceived as an indicator of a strengthening culture of liability. A possible goal for future studies is to undertake a comprehensive measurement of the popularity of both billing arrangements. The ratio of the popularity of billable hours to fee-for-service could serve as the basis for some sort of index of the culture of liability in China. We predict that as the value of the index increases and the culture of liability strengthens, Chinese lawyers will become more integrated into the business decision-making process and less frustrated by the role accorded to them by businessmen.

This chapter has attempted to give voice to the frustrations of Chinese lawyers. The intention here is not to cast Chinese lawyers as a bunch of complainers, nor is it to portray the Chinese legal system in a negative light. The fact of the matter is that certain problems do exist, and those problems will never be solved unless they can first be identified in an honest manner. To be even-handed, however, we must acknowledge that many problems have already been identified and solved. Over the course of the last thirty years, since the birth of the modern Chinese legal profession, amazing progress has been achieved. This chapter would not be complete without some recognition of that progress.

The rapid accumulation of human capital in the legal profession represents a tremendous achievement. In 1980 there were only a handful of educational institutions that taught law. Today there are hundreds. In 1980 there were only a few dozen people who were truly qualified to teach law. Today there are thousands. In 1980 there were roughly three thousand lawyers in the entire country.[17] Today there are roughly 121,000. In only thirty years, the bar has grown fortyfold! The expansion of the bar has been accompanied by the growth of a flourishing legal culture. Bar associations all around China offer to their members a full program of social and educational activities.[18] Lawyers and scholars have produced volumes of work on domestic legal culture and professional behavior.[19] In these thirty years, the Chinese legal profession has undergone a complete metamorphosis. Whereas thirty years ago, it was largely a fiction confined to the black and white of Five-Year Plans, today it is an animated reality.

Amazing achievements have also been made in the court of public opinion. The Chinese people have come to attribute great significance to the legal profession. Rather than relying on informal dispute-resolution mechanisms, Chinese people are more and more frequently turning to lawyers to resolve their disputes. All around China, there is a growing sense of rights consciousness. People are becoming accustomed to the idea that they are possessed of certain rights, and that lawyers are the key to enforcing those rights. According to several lawyers from Shanghai and Beijing, this is attributable to the media.[20] Law-related programs and documentaries are becoming more and more common on television. Newspapers increasingly report on the developments of important trials. As the popular culture has become saturated with talk of law and lawyers, the populace has come to regard them as tangible features of life that can be called upon in order to pursue their interests.

Finally, the Chinese legal profession has achieved something that the American legal profession has yet to attain: gender equality. In America, female lawyers are still an underrepresented minority. They still report a feeling of being trivialized in the classroom and restrained in the workplace. In China, female lawyers are anything but underrepresented. Female law students outnumber male law students.[21] Among judges who were recently elevated to the bench, females outnumber males. A survey was recently taken of lawyers in Shanghai under the age of thirty. Of the lawyers who earned ¥100,000 or more (the top income bracket), there were one-and-a-half times more females than males.[22] All of this is underscored by the fact that, nationally, males outnumber females by a sizable margin. Given the forgoing information, we must concede that the Chinese legal profession is considerably more gender progressive than the American legal profession.[23]

All of this progress must be taken into account when evaluating the overall disposition of the profession. Chinese lawyers are extremely proud of the progress that has been made, and rightly so. One female lawyer from Beijing commented very warmly on all of this progress: "So much of the lawyer system has improved over the last ten years, and I've been practicing all this time, and I feel like I have grown personally with the lawyer system."[24] Unquestionably, prominent problems still exist, and those problems must be addressed. We will probe several of those problems in the coming chapters. But in order to approach that undertaking with a level head, we must recognize the fact that the situation is not inert. On the contrary, profound advancements have taken place over the last thirty years.

CHAPTER 7

THE MARKET FOR CHINESE LAWYERS

The previous chapters have explored the history of lawyers in China, the relationship between lawyers and the rule of law, the channels for entry into the legal profession in China, the daily lives of Chinese lawyers, and the difficulties that they face in practicing law. Each of these topics dances around a central aspiration, which is the establishment of a nationwide network of lawyers for the purpose of promoting the rule of law. One could view the previous chapters as inquiries into the background, logic, means, status, and obstacles to fulfilling this aspiration. Having made inquiry into each of these topics, we now endeavor to take stock of our aspiration. Is there a nationwide network of lawyers? Is it adequate to promote the rule of law? In order to answer these questions, we must assess the market for Chinese lawyers. Our assessment of the market will include comments on the demand for Chinese lawyers, the supply of Chinese lawyers, the price of their time, and the organization of the industry. Following this, we will discuss the existence of several obstacles to a functioning market.

Demand

The demand for lawyers in China is small but growing. The types of legal services which are most highly demanded are telling indicators of the legal marketplace. The services which are in greatest demand are those that pertain to securities and financial law, initial public offerings, mergers and acquisitions, real estate transactions, and other areas of commerce. Other services, such as those that relate to family law, criminal law, personal injury law, and labor law, are in much less demand. It seems, in general, that the areas of law that pertain to the affairs of corporations are in greater demand than the areas of law that pertain to the affairs of people. It is interesting to note that services related to tax law are not very highly demanded, and the lawyers who specialize in tax law are considered low in status. A lawyer from Shanghai explained, "In America, tax law is one of the most complicated areas of law. In China, it is one of the least complicated areas. Because it's so easy and straightforward, lawyers are seldom needed to help file taxes."[1] This explanation, which was offered without any coaching or suggestion, sits favorably with the perspective explained in chapter 3, "The Rule of Law," which suggested that the longer and more specific a law is, the more difficult it will be to interpret the law without a specialized education, which creates demand for lawyers.

The demand for various legal services appears to be highly regionalized, with certain services being demanded in certain regions and not in others. In Beijing, the seat of the national government, much of the demand for lawyers revolves around interactions with the government, such as lobbying, competition for government contracts, and interactions with state-owned enterprises. For practical purposes, demand for these sorts of services does not exist outside of the Beijing legal market. In Shenzhen, the home of the Shenzhen Stock Exchange, much of the demand for lawyers revolves around securities law and initial public offerings. The same is true of Shanghai, which is home to China's largest stock exchange. Additionally, as the business capital of the country, much of the Shanghai legal market is focused on corporate law, international trade, and so forth. Outside of Shenzhen and Shanghai, the demand for legal services related to finance and commerce tapers off.

What about the rest of the country? Aside from those cities with territorial institutions, such as the stock market in Shanghai or the government in Beijing, it appears that there is no particular locus of demand in any area of law. Throughout the rest of the country, demand for legal services is anemic and scattered among different practice areas.

SUPPLY

A discussion of the supply of lawyers ought to begin by stating the size of the bar. Unfortunately, estimating the size of the bar in China is more of an art than a science. For one thing, official estimates of the size of the bar are published irregularly. Given the pace of change in China, estimates that are even one year old are unreliable. Secondly, official estimates of the size of the bar only reflect the number of licensed lawyers. But, there are many unlicensed individuals who provide legal services under the title of *consultant* rather than *lawyer*. It is unclear whether or not these people should be counted among the ranks of China's lawyers, even for the purposes of this discussion. Having made these disclaimers, as of 2006, the official number of lawyers in China was 121,889.[2] However, for the reasons listed above, we feel that this is an underrepresentation. Thus, we hold that the true number of lawyers in China is somewhere between one and two hundred thousand. To put this number into perspective, consider the following figures. Figure 1 shows the number of lawyers in each of several countries of different levels of economic development, figure 2 shows the number of lawyers per thousand citizens in each of those countries, and figure 3 shows the number of lawyers per hundred million dollars of GDP of each of those countries.[3] In absolute terms, China's lawyer population does not appear particularly small. It is greater than the lawyer populations of Australia, France, Turkey, and Canada. However, when one looks at the numbers proportionally, either in terms of lawyers per capita or lawyers per unit of economic output, it becomes clear that China's lawyer population is diminutive.

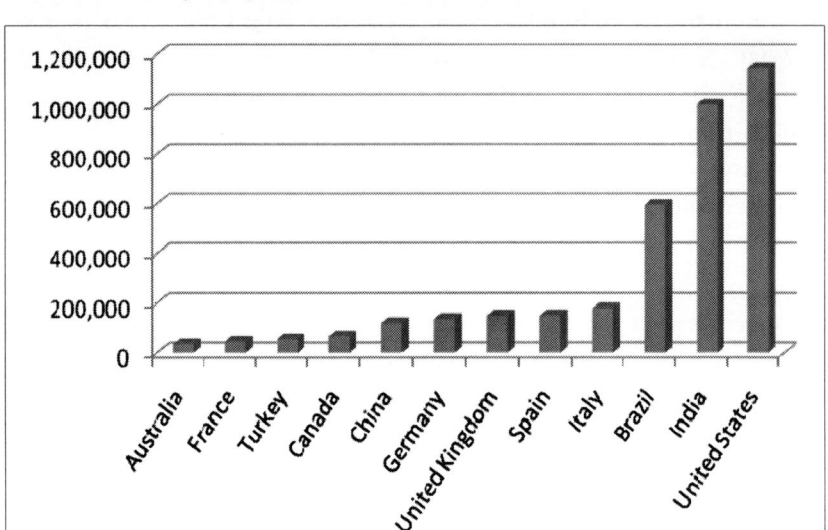

FIGURE 18. Lawyer populations in absolute terms.

Source. Adapted from Ordem dos Advogados do Brasil (2002), ABA Department of Market Research (2007), Benetton (2007), CCBE (2006), Canlaw (2009), Law Council of Australia (2004).

Relative to its population, France has seven times more lawyers than China. Relative to its population, the United Kingdom has twenty-seven times more lawyers than China. For every unit of economic output produced in Germany, there are three times more lawyers than in China. For every unit of economic output produced in the United States, there are four times more lawyers than in China. In other words, compared to the other countries shown in the charts above, there are significantly fewer lawyers involved in the lives and productive activities of the Chinese people. In chapter 3, "The Rule of Law," we established that there exists in China a widespread divergence between the demands of the law and the behavior of the people. Obviously, the people can only follow the law if they know what the law demands of them. How do the people come to know what the law demands of them? Generally speaking, such knowledge is conveyed by lawyers.

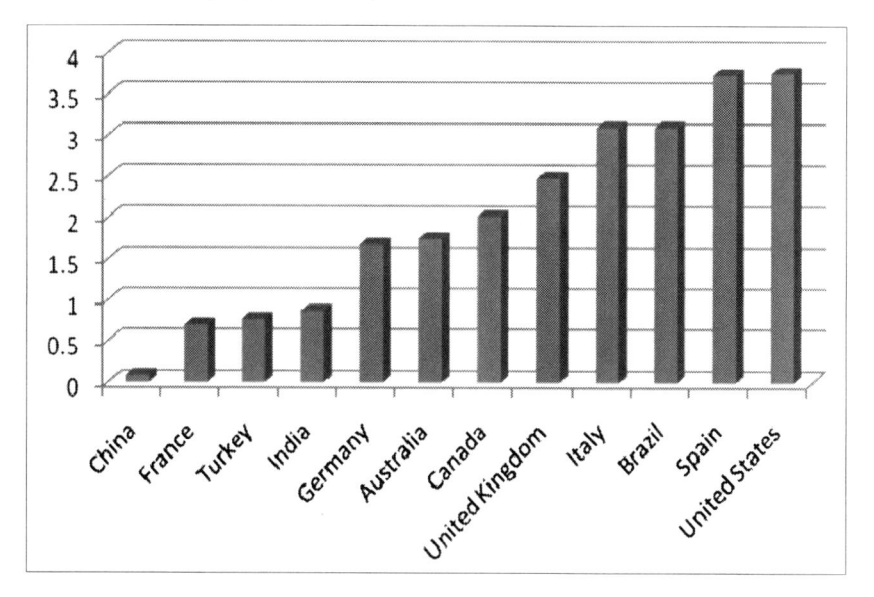

FIGURE 19. Lawyer populations per thousand citizens.

Source. Adapted from Ordem dos Advogados do Brasil (2002), ABA Department of Market Research (2007), Benetton (2007), CCBE (2006), Canlaw (2009), Law Council of Australia (2004), CIA World Factbook (2009).

This leads one to wonder, are there enough lawyers in the People's Republic of China to convey an effective understanding of what the law demands? Based on the number shown in the figures above, it appears unlikely.

The situation is even worse when one looks below the national level. The lawyers of China are tightly concentrated in a handful of large, economically developed cities along the eastern seaboard. The largest legal market is in Beijing, followed closely by Shanghai, and then Shenzhen, Nanjing, Guangzhou, and so on. The number of lawyers in Beijing exceeds ten thousand, as does the number of lawyers in Shanghai. This means that more than 16 percent of the total legal market is shared between those two cities, despite the fact that their population only comprises about 3 percent of the national total.

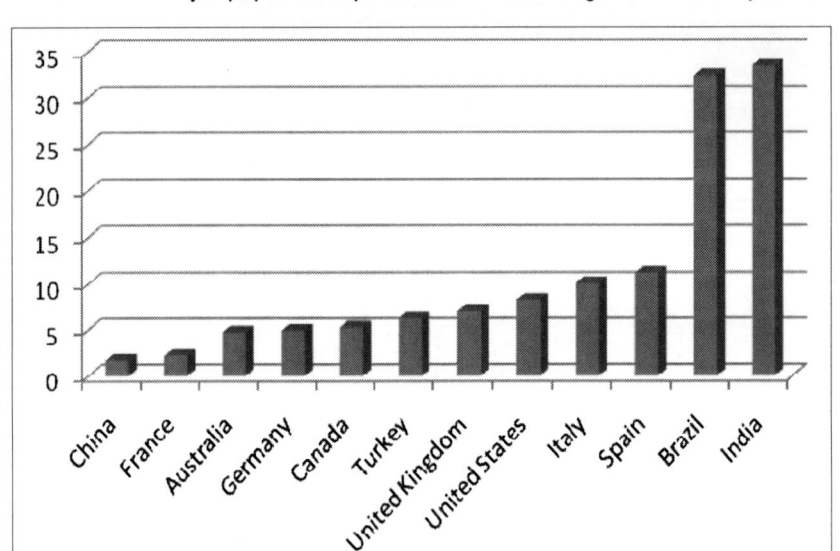

FIGURE 20. Lawyer populations per US$100 million of gross domestic product.

Source. Adapted from Ordem dos Advogados do Brasil (2002), ABA Department of Market Research (2007), Benetton (2007), CCBE (2006), Canlaw (2009), Law Council of Australia (2004), CIA World Factbook (2009).

The lopsided distribution of lawyers throughout the country means that the largest cities are very well served, but the less-developed areas are very poorly served:

> Yunnan province, a poor province in southwest China of roughly the same size and population as California, illustrates this problem. The entire province has only 2,782 lawyers providing legal services for a population of 44 million people. In sharp contrast, the state of California has 155,992 lawyers, which is more than the bar registration of all of China. Of comparable note, Guizhou, one of China's poorest provinces, with a population of almost 40 million, has only about 1,400 lawyers.[4]

The low number of lawyers in some areas is certainly problematic. But even more problematic is the fact that some areas have no lawyers whatsoever. According to the 2000 census, there are 2,053 counties in China.[5] As of 2006, there were 206 counties that did not have a single lawyer.[6] This means that approximately 10 percent of the legal jurisdictions in China are completely devoid of lawyers! How can the residents of these jurisdictions know what the law demands of them when there is nobody present to explain it to them? And, even if they did know the demands of the law, what if they decided to contravene those demands? If someone in one these jurisdictions decided to set up a counterfeiting operation, would there be anybody around to object? If you were a counterfeiter, would you rather set up shop around Beijing or would you rather set up shop in one of these jurisdictions?

The incredibly lopsided distribution of lawyers is a topic of critical importance, which will be taken up in depth later in this chapter. For now, we will merely point out that the lopsided distribution of lawyers makes it impossible to say anything comprehensive about *the Chinese legal market*. There is no such thing as *the Chinese legal market*. The market in a location like Yunnan is so radically different from the market in a location like Beijing that it makes absolutely no sense to try to paint them both with the same brush. Bearing this point in mind, we will attempt to convey some understanding of what a Chinese lawyer's time is worth.

COMPENSATION

Lawyer's billing rates are regulated by the Lawyers Services Fee Collection Regulation Law, which was promulgated on September 1, 2006.[7] The worth of a Chinese lawyer's time appears to be valued at anywhere between ¥200 and ¥2,000 per hour, which equates to roughly $30 to $300 per hour. Just as in the West, the price of a lawyer's time varies substantially with the prestige of the firm for which the lawyer works, the type of work being performed, and the lawyer's credentials, such as education and experience. Also as in the West, the amount that a lawyer charges per hour is not equivalent to the amount that the lawyer earns per hour. The amount that the lawyer earns, which is some fraction of what he charges, is determined largely by his seniority in the firm. The more senior a lawyer is, the greater the fraction of his hourly rate he can keep for himself. The more junior a lawyer is, the greater the fraction of his hourly rate must be turned over to the firm.

In 2006 a survey was taken of lawyers in Shanghai under the age of thirty.[8] The lawyers were asked to indicate if their annual income was between ¥10,000 and ¥50,000, between ¥50,000 and ¥100,000, or greater than ¥100,000. The results of the survey are shown in the graph below. Based on the exchange rate at the time of writing, ¥10,000 is roughly equivalent to $1,400, ¥50,000 is roughly equivalent to $7,000, and ¥100,000 is roughly equivalent to $14,000. However, because the cost of living in China is significantly lower than in the West, the official exchange rate is not a good measure of assessing the value of income. To get a sense of the value of these income levels, one should note that in 2007, the average income in urban China was ¥24,932.[9] An income of ¥100,000 in China can support the same sort of lifestyle as an income of $100,000 in America.

This graph provides some sense of a lawyer's earning power in Shanghai. Bear in mind, however, that Shanghai is not only one of the top legal markets in China, but it is also the most economically developed city, with the highest cost of living. Given this, it would be a mistake to presume that all lawyers in China earn these sorts of incomes. As explained earlier, it is almost impossible to make nationwide generalizations about the Chinese legal market. The one exception appears to be the 80/20 rule. All Chinese lawyers in every part of the country speak of the 80/20 rule. The 80/20 rule says that 80 percent of the lawyers in a given location will earn only 20 percent of the income, and the remaining 20 percent of the lawyers in that location will earn the remaining 80 percent of the income. When asked about income distribution within the field, all Chinese lawyers respond by reciting this rule. The perfect harmony of their recitation almost leads one to question its legitimacy. But whether or not it is legitimate, the fact that lawyers everywhere believe it to be legitimate is an important fact in and of itself. This means that the average lawyer does not expect to earn a great deal of money. Rather, the

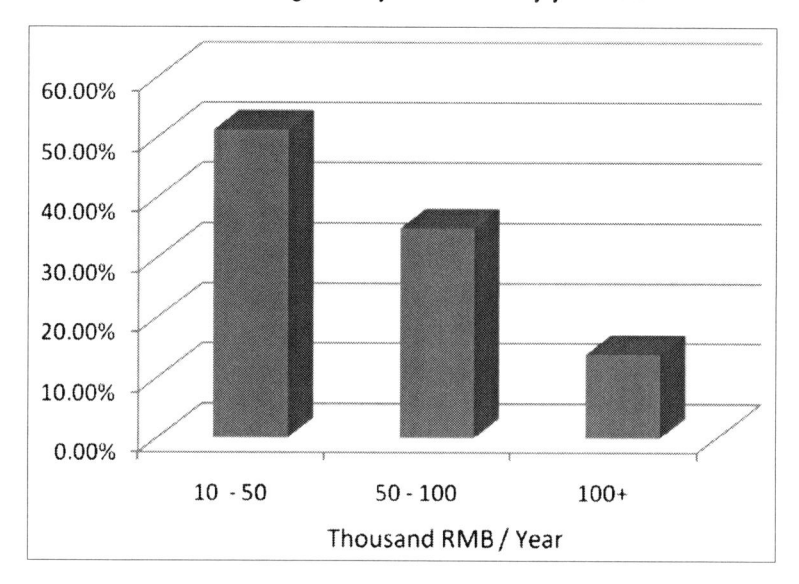

FIGURE 21. Income of Shanghai lawyers under thirty years old.

Source. Adapted from Young Lawyers Committee (2006).

average lawyer expects to barely make ends meet while a small coterie of his colleagues grows fabulously wealthy. Based on our interviews, this expectation appears to be more or less well founded.

FIRM ORGANIZATION

The means of organizing legal enterprise in China is an interesting departure from the West. In the West, law firms tend to be very large, with hierarchical chains of authority. The firm is divided up into different practice areas, with partners and associates in each area. The partners of each area work in concert with the partners of the other areas; the associates of each area, however, focus narrowly on the work of their own area. The partners are largely responsible for attracting business to the firm, while the associates are responsible for undertaking the work of each case. This model of organizing a law firm is referred to as the *corporatized law firm model*, or the *finders and grinders model*. This model is not an accident of modern conditions. Rather, this model developed organically from the practice of apprenticeship and the structure of legal guilds in traditional Western society. Thus, the corporatized law firm model is intimately related to Western culture.

Although the terminology of the corporatized law firm model (*partner, associate*) has been transplanted into China, the corporatized law firm model itself is very uncommon. There are only a handful of firms in the largest cities that are organized in this way. Most firms in China have very loose, horizontal organization.[10] In each firm, there are several experienced lawyers, and each experienced lawyer has a crew of junior lawyers working under him. Each crew will engage in many types of legal practice; specialization is uncommon. The experienced lawyer is concerned primarily with attracting business to the crew, not to the firm. It is very common for crews within the same firm to have separate accounting. The leaders of crews rarely work in concert with one another; sometimes they have no interaction whatsoever. For this reason, when referring to the experienced lawyers in Chinese firms, we consider the term *partner* to be a misnomer.

The way in which law firms in China are typically organized is quite reminiscent of *gong tou* (工头), which means "work head." The term *gong tou* refers to an early Chinese capitalist who would employ many young, able-bodied workers to perform all manner of manual labor. The *gong tou* would find business opportunities to capitalize on and then sit back, watching in comfort as his workers created wealth on his behalf. There is some connotation of exploitation associated with *gong tou*. The *gong tou* was an independent entrepreneur, unaccustomed to working in partnership with other *gong tou*. Because of the apparent parallels, we refer to the model of law firm organization which is dominant in China as the *gong tou model*.

When asked why the *gong tou* model is so much more prevalent than the corporatized law firm model, interview subjects responded that the work performed by most law firms is not so demanding or so sophisticated as to require the involvement of large teams of people from many different specialties. Thus, the *gong tou* model is adequate to meet the needs of their clients. As the size and complexity of legal work in China grows, we expect that the corporatized law firm model will become more common.

OBSTACLES TO A FUNCTIONING MARKET

There are between one hundred and two hundred thousand lawyers in China. There is demand for legal services all around the country, particularly in the large cities. Where there exists demand and supply, there should exist a market to connect demanders with suppliers and mete out a price. There does exist a market in China to connect demanders of legal services with suppliers of legal services; however, the market is not functioning smoothly. In this section, we will identify two obstacles to a functioning market for legal services in China.

The first obstacle is the lack of a nationwide legal directory. In America, for example, the Martindale legal directory lists the name, contact information, educational background, and specialty of every lawyer and law firm in the country. This allows a lawyer in Los Angeles to interact seamlessly with a lawyer in Chicago, a firm in New York to establish a cooperative relationship with a firm in Miami, and a litigant in rural North Dakota to contact all four parties to determine who is best situated to represent his case. This sort of directory provides all suppliers of legal services and all demanders of legal services with total information awareness, breaks down the physical barriers that separate various parties, and simulates the existence of a single, unified marketplace for legal services. By contrast, there is no such directory in China. If an individual in Beijing needs to hire a lawyer to represent his interests in Gansu Province, he must physically travel to Gansu to locate a lawyer, or find an advertisement on the Internet, or rely on word of mouth. Assuming there is only one occasion in this individual's life in which he needs to represent his interests in a distant location, then this process would merely constitute a great hassle. But if this individual is engaged in nationwide commerce and frequently needs to represent his interests in a variety of distant locations, then this problem will become prohibitive. The lack of a nationwide legal directory impairs the ability of suppliers and demanders of legal services to come together in the market.

The second obstacle to a functioning market for Chinese lawyers is the obstructed flow of human capital. Upon birth, every Chinese citizen is issued a certificate, or *hukou* (户口), that lists the individual's biographical information and location of their parents' residency. The rights and services that the government provides for the people, such as public education and free health care, are only effective in the location that is listed on the individual's *hukou*. Additionally, the individual's permanent educational and employment records, called a personnel file, or *renshi dangan* (人事档案), are stored at a local government agency called the Local Labor Agency, or *cundang jigou* (存档机构).[11] Each employer has the responsibility of maintaining the personnel files of all of its employees, and that responsibility is transferred from one employer to another when an employee changes jobs. When an individual wishes to relocate to a job in a new city, he must request for his personnel file to be conveyed from the Local Labor Agency to the Local Labor Agency in the new city. If the individual then wishes to relocate to a third city, the personnel file must be routed back to the original Local Labor Agency before it can be sent to the Local Labor Agency of the third city. In effect, an individual's personnel file is forever domiciled in his hometown, and can only be sent out to other cities on loan. These files are necessary for everything, from applying for a job to applying for a library card. As a result, the procedural hassles of the personnel file system create a significant impediment to relocating in pursuit of career opportunities.

The combined effect of the personnel file system and the *hukou* system is essentially to tie the individual down to his or her parents' hometown. In many cases, this is undesirable because China's development has been extremely lopsided. The large cities have developed much faster than the small villages, and the provinces on the eastern seaboard have developed much faster than the inland provinces. If an individual's *hukou* is registered to a large city on the eastern seaboard, then that individual is entitled to all of the riches and opportunities of that city. On the other hand, if an individual's *hukou* is registered to a rural town in central China, then the standard of living and level of opportunities of the individual are quite limited. The only possibility of improving one's lot is to apply for a temporary residency permit in a big city. These permits, however, are infrequently awarded. Thus, the *hukou* system is problematic because it interrupts the free flow of human capital.

This problem is relevant to everyone, but it is particularly relevant to law students in the less-developed provinces. As stated earlier, there is very little demand for lawyers outside of the largest cities. However, many law schools are located outside of the largest cities. For graduates of these law schools, the prospects are bleak. If they stay in the less-developed province, the likelihood is that they will be unable to find a job as a lawyer and their education will go to waste. One lawyer from the countryside hoping to find work in the city explained the attitude held by people in her situation: "I am a graduate of a great law school; how can I go back to my hometown where there are just farms? What would I do there?"[12] On the other hand, if they apply for a residency permit in a big city, it is unlikely that their application will be approved. The chances of approval are increased significantly if the application is sponsored by a prestigious law firm in the city. However, in order for the applicant to convince a law firm to sponsor her, she must distinguish herself from all of the other lawyers that are eager to move to the city to avoid languishing in the provinces. For those lawyers with superior education, they can distinguish themselves on the basis of credentials. But, as with anything, only a few people can be superior.

For the average many, how can they distinguish themselves? They can only distinguish themselves on the basis of price. By indicating a willingness to accept substandard pay, they can make themselves attractive to the big-city firms. This shortchanges the applicant's true value and is harmful not only to that individual applicant but to all applicants, whether they are from the countryside or the city. If there is a steady stream of applicants who are willing to work for less and less money in order to circumvent an artificially imposed migration control, then it will be nearly impossible to establish a salary floor that supports a decent standard of living.

Additionally, the *hukou* system promotes a brain-drain from the provinces to the cities. High school students in the provinces who perform exceedingly well on the college entrance exam will be admitted to prestigious universities in the large cities, whereupon they will be granted de facto residency. The students who remain in the provinces for college are second-rate talent. But even among the second-rate, some will perform better than others. College students in the provinces who rise to the top of their law classes will be best positioned to persuade prestigious urban law firms to sponsor their applications for temporary residency. If their applications are approved, they will move to the city, and the talent pool in the provinces shrinks again. As a result of this dynamic, many of the law students who remain in the provinces to practice law after graduation are third-rate talent.

Further complicating the matter, there is not even enough demand for legal services in the provinces to employ all of the third-rate talent. One lawyer from Jiangsu Province, who had successfully made the transition to Shanghai, related that of all of her classmates from graduate school, nearly half had left the legal profession within one year because there were no law jobs available in Jiangsu.[13] This anecdote raises the question, why are there so many more law students in the provinces than law jobs? Is the supply of law students too high, or is the demand for lawyers too low? If the answer is that the supply of law students is too high, then we must ask why so many students in the provinces choose to study law despite the bleak job prospects. On the other hand, if the answer is that the demand for lawyers is too low, then we must ask why it is so low and what can be done to stimulate it.

According to Yu Zong, author of *In the Shadow of the Statute of Liberty*, the popularity of studying law stems not from the market demand for lawyers or the job prospects at the time of matriculation, but rather from the popular wisdom that "China needs more lawyers."[14] In the event that popular wisdom catches up to reality, that is to say, acknowledges the bleak job prospects for law graduates, then there is a danger that the momentum will subside and the growth of the legal profession will derail. This explains the disconnect between supply and demand, but it does not explain why the demand is so low. If you add up the number of residents of the one hundred largest cities in China, the total does not even exceed 250 million people.[15] This means that there are more than one billion people living in the smaller cities, towns, and villages all around China. It's not as though a billion people are just sitting on their hands. On the contrary, there are countless farms, enterprises, and production facilities in these areas. Given all of the trillions of personal interactions and commercial transactions of a billion people, it stands to reason that somebody would want to hire a lawyer. And, in fact, some people do want to hire lawyers, but not nearly as many as one would expect.

There are cultural factors at play. Chinese culture prizes tranquility; there is a stigma against being involved in a dispute. Thus, people are reluctant to get involved in litigation, even when they have good reason to do so. In addition to cultural mores, there is a very practical reason to avoid litigation. Because of the *hukou* system, people must conduct themselves on the assumption that their current community will be their community for life. Given this assumption, there is a high premium on cultivating a good reputation. People avoid litigation, at least in part, because they do not want to acquire a reputation for being confrontational with their long-term neighbors. Aversion to litigation is a large part of the reason why demand for lawyers in the provinces is so low. But what about other legal services aside from litigation? Why aren't those in demand?

Based on hundreds of hours of interviews with lawyers all around China, we have come to the conclusion that the anemic demand for lawyers in the provinces is principally attributable to the weak culture of liability. People and enterprises in the provinces are simply not very concerned with the possible legal consequences of their actions. This is not to say that they are bad people; on the contrary, they tend to be very wholesome folks. In some cases, they've simply never heard of the concept of legal consequences. In other cases, it is because they do not know that their own actions might carry legal consequences. In other cases still, it is because they do not believe that the consequences of their actions will ever catch up with them. No matter what the reason is, it boils down to a matter of expectations. If someone has an expectation that she will be held accountable for the consequences of her actions, she will be concerned with liability. If someone does not have an expectation that she will be held accountable for the consequences of her actions, she will not be concerned with liability. It's as simple as that. No matter what the state of economic development is or how many big businesses there are, the demand for lawyers in the provinces will only be stimulated when there is a widespread expectation among the people of the provinces that they will be held accountable for the legal consequences of their actions.

Conclusion

The purpose of this chapter was to deliberate a question of singular importance: is there a nationwide network of lawyers for the promotion of the rule of law? The critical terms in this question are *nationwide*, *network*, and *promotion*. Given that 10 percent of the legal jurisdictions of China do not have any lawyers in them, the term *nationwide* is unsuitable. Given the absence of a national legal directory, the term *network* is unsuitable. And given that the majority of citizens live in effective isolation from the majority of lawyers, it seems unlikely that much *promotion* is possible. Thus, we find that China does not yet possess a nationwide network of lawyers for the promotion of the rule of law, but it surely needs one.

The lack of a nationwide network of lawyers should not be blamed on the lawyers themselves. They are not the problem; they are the solution. But neither should the blame be placed upon the government. The government is doing the best job that it can, given the circumstances. The government is spending a fortune to send law students abroad for advanced legal training, to endow new law schools all around the country, and to invest in improving the judiciary. The government has enacted numerous policies designed to promote the legal profession. We believe that the intentions are very sincere, even if imperfectly implemented. We will not indulge in asking who is to blame. Rather, we will ask what can be done to improve the situation. The next chapter will propose a platform of policy recommendations designed to help establish a nationwide network of lawyers for the promotion of the rule of law.

CHAPTER 8

POLICY RECOMMENDATIONS

The principal objective of this book is to describe the current condition of lawyers in China. The secondary objective of this book is to suggest policies to improve the condition of lawyers in China. The first objective was undertaken impartially, without any bias or agenda. However, as soon as one begins to undertake the second objective, the air of impartiality is immediately compromised. The wording of the second objective—to improve the condition of lawyers in China—is only logical if one starts with a defined sense of what constitutes improvement, and for whom. In light of this peril, we will make our best effort to preserve a balanced perspective and limit our policy recommendations to those which can clearly be justified as achieving universally desirable outcomes.

The foremost problem that this chapter will treat is the anemic demand for lawyers. The great Communist scholar E. P. Thompson once wrote that the rule of law is "an unqualified human good."[1] Based on all of the ideas laid out in chapter 3, as well as Thompson's bona fides as a scholar and a leading member of the Communist Party, we assert that cultivating the rule of law in China is a universally desirable goal. However, as long as there are large tracts of the country that have no lawyers or too few lawyers, there will always be legions of people who are, at best, unresponsive to the law, and, at worst, serious criminals. Whether or not there are enough lawyers in the large cities is a debatable question, but an irrelevant one, because anyone who wishes to consciously violate the law will have a motive to relocate to an area with a diminutive lawyer population. In other words, the chain of the rule of law is only as strong as its weakest link. From this perspective, it is exceedingly evident that China needs more lawyers.

Just how many more lawyers does China need? In the previous chapter, three charts were shown which displayed the number of lawyers, size of the population, and size of the economy for each of several countries. If we assume that the number of lawyers in each of those countries is appropriate to promote the rule of law (which, admittedly, is a big assumption), then we can make an educated guess about the number of lawyers that China needs by calculating how many lawyers the other countries *would* need, on average, if their populations and economies were as large as China's. After crunching some statistics, we arrive at a figure of 1,440,281.[2] Assuming that the current real number of lawyers is 121,889, then in order to be on an equal footing with the other countries, China needs about 1.3 million more lawyers.

The exact number is guesswork, but the bottom line is that China needs many, many more lawyers in order to support the rule of law. Recruiting and cultivating that many lawyers will not be possible under the current conditions of anemic demand. Therefore, it is the position of this book that the government should undertake actions designed to stimulate demand for lawyers. As explained in the previous chapter, the most fundamental cause of the feeble demand for lawyers is the weak culture of liability. The farther away from the big cities you go, the less people expect to be held accountable for the legal consequences of their actions. The government should strengthen the culture of liability by *providing the people of the provinces with a reason to expect to be held accountable* for the legal consequences of their actions. This concept is a bit difficult to communicate, so we will explain in detail what exactly is meant.

Normally, the most qualified, tenacious, and intelligent law students go from university directly into jobs at top firms in the largest cities. We propose a program to harness the patriotism and talent of those students in order to better their country. We propose to recruit those students to take public-interest positions at legal-aid clinics and prosecutors' offices in the smaller cities, villages, and countryside for a period of two years. Normally, those students would never consider such options because they would not be financially competitive with the offers that they would receive from the top firms, and because it would jeopardize their future career trajectory. But imagine if they *would* take such options. Imagine the consequences that would follow from diverting some of the top legal talent of the generation to go out into the provinces to prosecute all manner of violations in the name of building the rule of law. These would be lawyers on a mission. These would be lawyers of the highest caliber and diligence. These would be lawyers who have no stake in the local economy and bear no lasting allegiance to the local political order. Free of such encumbrances and emboldened by the reputation of the program, these young lawyers would have no hesitation about pursuing legitimate violations of the law wherever they can be found. Observing the storm of prosecution, the people of the provinces would seek shelter. They would grow to expect to be held accountable for the legal consequences of their actions. As a result, they would take a greater interest in managing their exposure to liability, and their demand for legal services would increase. With each year that passes and each new class of lawyers that arrives, the culture of liability would strengthen and demand for legal services would grow. After a few years, it would develop its own momentum. This is the logic of the program that we propose.

The two issues that remain to be discussed are the means of recruiting the top law students into the program and the impact that the program would have on the provinces. First, we shall discuss the approach to recruitment. As stated earlier, the best law graduates are disinclined to take public-interest positions in the provinces because such positions are not financially competitive with offers from top firms in the big cities, and because of the likelihood that such a choice would damage their career trajectory. In order to ameliorate the concern about career trajectory, the program must be promoted as an elite and honorable career launching pad. In this regard, the program should be modeled after Teach for America, which has been very successful in creating such an image. Many of America's most talented college graduates are willing to postpone their professional ambitions to join Teach for America. Undoubtedly, this willingness is founded on altruism. But altruism is strongly supplemented by the fact that Teach for America is considered to be a prestigious program. Students who join Teach for America expect that upon completion of the program, they will have a leg up on applying to elite jobs and graduate schools. This expectation is well founded. Teach for America has formal partnerships with hundreds of top employers and universities, all of whom have agreed to confer an assortment of benefits on alumni of Teach for America. In order to ameliorate the concerns that Chinese law students have about career trajectory, the program would need to cultivate a similar reputation.

In order to ameliorate the concerns about financial competitiveness, the program would offer a debt-forgiveness incentive: if a participant agrees to hold a public-interest position in the provinces for two years, then all of the debt that they accumulated in law school will be forgiven. Of course, the institution that owned the student's debt will have lost money, so the government must compensate the institution with some resource of equal value. Thankfully, the Chinese government is not short on resources. In addition to untold billions of dollars' worth of Chinese currency held in reserve, the foreign currency reserves of the government exceed $1.6 trillion. The amount of money needed to finance this program pales in comparison. Depending on the number of students participating each year and the average tuition level, the cost of financing this program would fall somewhere between $10 and $20 million per year. To put this number in perspective, the amount of money that the Chinese government spent to prepare for the Olympics is upwards of $40 billion. The opening ceremony alone cost $300 million! If one evening of entertainment is worth $300 million, then a lifetime of order is certainly worth $20 million. If a sporting event that lasts for two weeks is worth $40 billion, then surely building the rule of law is worth $20 million.

The only issue that remains to be addressed is the impact that this program would have on the provinces. If the demand for lawyers in the provinces is to increase, clearly this will come at the expense of the people of the provinces: they will have to devote a greater share of their resources to paying lawyer fees. At first glance, this may appear inhumane. After all, many of the poorest people in China reside in the provinces, the average income level in the provinces is markedly lower than in the cities, and the economies of the provinces are underdeveloped. Given these facts, how could one justify saddling these people with lawyer bills? If you look more closely, however, and consider the nuances of the situation, it's not really so bad. An individual's interest in hiring a lawyer is a function of the individual's exposure to liability. Most often, significant exposure to liability is a result of significant involvement in commerce. In other words, the greatest increase in demand for lawyers would come from the people who are most capable of bearing the expense, not from the people who are starving in the streets. Furthermore, the economies of the provinces are developing, and the pace of development is increasing. The rising cost of land and labor in the cities is driving many urban enterprises to relocate to the provinces. As the economies of the provinces grow, there are more and more resources available. Some of these resources could, and rightly should, be devoted to building the rule of law. Nonetheless, if it appears that this program would place too great of a financial burden on the people of the provinces, the government could offset this burden with some sort of tax rebate. The bottom line is that the provinces are poised to develop, and the people of the provinces will enjoy greater prosperity than ever before imagined. Everyone, Chinese or otherwise, should look favorably upon this. Lifting hundreds of millions of people out of poverty is an achievement that benefits the whole of humanity. While we look favorably on the prospect of this achievement, we must make sure that it is done responsibly. Neither the people of the provinces nor the people of the world benefit from the spread of Wild West–style capitalism. For this reason, we strongly recommend that the government take action to stimulate demand for legal services beyond the largest cities.

The second problem that this chapter will address is the *kan hao* system (see chapter 6—"Frustrations in the Practice of Law"). As a result of the prevailing quota, the limited availability of *kan haos* has a debilitating effect on lawyers and a rotting effect on academia. In order to solve this problem, the government need only eliminate the quota. There is nothing technically challenging about allowing more *kan haos* to be issued. A *kan hao* is nothing more than a series of numbers and letters, roughly ten digits long. An example of a *kan hao* from one Chinese law journal is CN31-2008/D. In an age of digital processing and mass computerization, there is no plausible reason to believe that the apparatus which manages the distribution of publications could not handle more digits. Thus, there is no technical obstacle to liberalizing or eliminating the quota. Whatever other objections might exist to eliminating the quota cannot possibly be justified given the retarding effect that it has on law and academia. On this basis, we recommend that the government eliminate the quota for *kan haos*.

The last problem that this chapter will address is barriers to information. One such barrier is the absence of a nationwide legal directory, and another is the absence of an affordable, comprehensive, online legal-research platform. Both of these shortcomings should be corrected in order to enable the free flow of information needed to create an effective legal market. The nationwide legal directory would be quite easy to create because the infrastructure for frequent contact with the entire legal community is already in place. Every lawyer in the country must submit an application to the local bureau of justice each year to renew her lawyer's license. At the time of renewal, the applicants could be compelled to report their current place of employment, contact information, specialty, and so on. This information could easily be compiled into a nationwide legal directory at very little expense. Given that this problem lends itself to a government solution, we recommend that the government take responsibility for the creation of a nationwide legal directory.

While addressing the absence of a nationwide legal directory will be straightforward, it will be more challenging to address the absence of an affordable, comprehensive, online legal-research platform. There is a comprehensive online legal-research platform called Beida Fabao, which was created by a public research institution affiliated with Beijing University. However, almost nobody subscribes because the price of a subscription is prohibitively expensive. The government should establish a working group to study this problem. The first question that the working group should consider is whether the provision of a legal resource of this nature should be the domain of the public or private sector. What is the nature of such a resource? If access to the law is only available through a government institution, does this imply some sort of discontinuity between the citizen and the law? If so, is this sort of discontinuity compatible with the ambition of transforming the law into a tangible presence in the daily lives of the people? If the working group concludes that it should be the domain of the public sector, then it must investigate why the current price is so high and what options are available to bring the price into range with the value that consumers set on this service. After all, the mere existence of such a service is not enough to have an impact; the service must be practically accessible. If, on the other hand, the working group concludes that the creation of a comprehensive online legal-research platform should be the domain of the private sector, then it must deliberate why the private sector has not already created a comprehensive platform, what sorts of obstacles stand in the way, and what types of incentives the government could use in order to overcome these obstacles. The working group could draw expertise through consultation with LexisNexis, Westlaw, and other foreign providers of online legal-research platforms. Given that this project is relatively challenging, we recommend that the government prioritize the formation of a working group to study the task of creating a comprehensive online legal-research platform.

The forgoing remarks are a brief description of some of the policy measures that should be considered in order to improve the condition of Chinese lawyers. This is by no means an exhaustive list—there are many other, smaller measures which could be taken. For example, many courts do not have a court reporter. Justice tends to be sloppy when it is not recorded. There are many pieces of equipment that should be, but are not, standard issue in every courthouse. The salaries of judges may be suboptimal, and the tables used to calculate the salaries of court employees (including judges) are complicated and confusing, which makes it very easy to conceal bribery. All of these matters must be considered when determining what policies should be implemented to soothe the frustrations of Chinese lawyers and cultivate the bar into a force for the promotion of the rule of law. All of these matters merit thorough investigation. This study, however, will rest upon the four recommendations highlighted in bold font. These recommendations stand in a position of paramount importance. They are critical to improving the condition of Chinese lawyers, promoting the rule of law, and extending the reach of governance across the entire country. In short, they are indispensable to governing China beyond the mandate of heaven.

Conclusion

Beyond the Mandate of Heaven

The goal of this book was to explore frustrations in and about China, with the aim of forging an understanding as to whether the uncertainty, disorder, and lack of accountability that characterize life in modern China might emanate from the current stature of its legal profession. In this process, we have identified two landmark changes that have occurred in China over the past two hundred years. The first major change is the wholesale casting off of all things traditional. This includes the traditional understanding of China's role in the world, traditional culture, the classics, and the mandate of heaven. The elimination of these forces, which formerly endowed Chinese society with order, has generated enormous shockwaves that have reverberated throughout the generations.

The second major change is the building of a modern economy. The form, scope, and scale of production have undergone an unprecedented degree of change. By *form of production*, we mean what sorts of goods and services are produced. By *scope of production*, we mean how widely those goods and services are distributed. And by *scale of production*, we mean how much of each good and service is produced. Gone are the days when China's economy consisted of subsistence agriculture and handicrafts such as silk and porcelain. Today, China manufactures frozen foods, broadband routers, and sophisticated pharmaceuticals.

No longer are the goods and services consumed by an individual produced within a few kilometers of that individual's village, where everyone within the village shared some degree of kinship with everyone else and some sense of responsibility to everyone else. Today, Chinese goods are sent all around the country, from Dalian to Xinjiang, and around the world, from Shanghai to Santa Monica. Production no longer occurs at a mere arm's length away. With the consumer out of sight, responsibility is out of mind.

Changes in the form and scope of production are exceeded only by changes in the scale of production. Between 1978 and 2007, the economy grew almost fifteenfold.[1] There is fifteen times more productive activity occurring today than there was in 1978. There are fifteen times more temptations to cut corners today than there were in 1978. In order to assure the fulfillment of obligations and the defense of rights, there must be something on the order of fifteen times more oversight and enforcement today than there was in 1978. As we learned in chapter 3, "The Rule of Law," oversight and enforcement in China are provided by a mix of public action by bureaucrats and private action by lawyers. Between 1978 and 2003, the state's share of the economy was reduced from 80 percent to less than 20 percent.[2] As the government's involvement in the economy is reduced, the government's own ability to provide oversight and enforcement in and via the realm of production is necessarily diminished.

Bearing all of this in mind, it is clear that the growth of the legal profession has not kept adequate pace to simultaneously match the growth of productive activity and compensate for the government's diminished capacity as overseer and enforcer. We have shown that oversight and enforcement are provided in sufficient amounts by neither the government, nor the lawyers, nor the classics, nor any other perceivable source.

As a result, significant amounts of productive activity take place under conditions of low-level anarchy. This phenomenon is responsible for the sensations of uncertainty, disorder, and lack of accountability that characterize much of life in China today.

In the process of undertaking this exploration, we have seen that the major trends in the legal profession have always been stimulated by China's choppy relationship with the outside world. The profession originally emerged to accommodate the demands of European traders who were unwelcome guests on Chinese soil. The profession was then purged because of its relationship to a political regime that was considered too friendly with the West, then again because the profession was too enthusiastic about ideas of governance that were foreign in origin, then again because of the depravities of a man who perceived phantom threats of capitalists, spies, and saboteurs around every corner. Finally, the profession was revived in order to coax foreign firms to invest in Chinese enterprises. A review of this history indicates that the legal profession has always been driven by and focused on China's relationship with the outside world. This view is substantiated by the fact that, in nearly every law school, the most popular courses have names like "International Economic Law" and "Legal English."[3] This view is further substantiated by Chinese popular wisdom, such as the expression *ren pa guan, guan pa yang* (人怕官官怕洋), which means "the people fear officials, the officials fear foreigners."

We conclude this book by asking when the legal profession will no longer be driven by foreign relations alone, but by domestic relations as well. When will the legal profession be focused as much on the rights of Chinese citizens as on the rights of foreign investors? We look forward with eagerness to the day when the legal profession is not just *of* the Chinese people, but *for* the Chinese people. For on that day, China will truly pass beyond the mandate of heaven.

Appendix A
Chinese Law Schools

Beijing

Beijing University, Qinghua University, Renmin University of China, Beijing Normal University, Beijing University of Science and Technology, Northern Jiaotong University, Beijing Polytechnic University, Beijing University of Aeronautics and Astronautics, Beijing Chemical Industry University, China Agricultural University, the University of Petroleum, the Foreign Trade and Economic University, the Central University for Nationalities, China University of Geosciences, China University of Politics and Law, the Chinese People's Public Security University, Central University of Finance and Economics, Beijing Union University, North China University of Technology, Beijing University of Commerce and Industry, the China Youth Political College, the Foreign Affairs College, Beijing Agricultural College, China's Civil Aviation College

Tianjin

Nankai University and Tianjin University, Tianjin Normal University, Tianjin Business School, Tianjin University, Tianjin Institute of Finance and Economics, Tianjin Medical University

Hebei

Hebei University, North China Electric Power University, Hebei Normal University, Yanshan University, Hebei Economic and

Trade University, School of Economics, Shijiazhuang, Hebei University of Science and Technology, Shijiazhuang Railway Institute

SHANXI

Taiyuan University of Technology, Shanxi University, Shanxi University of Finance and Economics, Taiyuan Heavy Machinery Institute

INNER MONGOLIA

University of Inner Mongolia, Inner Mongolia Institute of Finance and Economics

LIAONING

Northeastern University, Liaoning University, Dalian Maritime University, Northeast University of Finance and Economics, Shenyang Industrial University, Liaoning Engineering Technology University, Liaoning Normal University, Shenyang Normal University, Teachers College, Jinzhou, Anshan Iron and Steel Institute

JILIN

Jilin University, Yanbian University, Northeast Normal University, Changchun Institute of Optical Precision Machinery, Jilin Engineering Institute, the Changchun Institute of Taxation

HEILONGJIANG

Harbin Institute of Technology, Harbin Engineering University, Heilongjiang University, Northeast Forestry University, the

University of Qiqihar, Harbin University of Business, the Harbin Normal University

SHANGHAI

Fudan University, Shanghai Jiaotong University, Tongji University, East China Normal University, Donghua University, Shanghai University, Shanghai International Studies University, Shanghai University of Finance and Economics, Shanghai Shipping Institute, Shanghai Institute of Foreign Trade, the East China College of Political Science and Law

JIANGSU

Nanjing University, Soochow University, Southeast University, Hehai University, China University of Mining, Nanjing Polytechnic University, Southern Yangtze University, Nanjing University of Aeronautics and Astronautics, Nanjing Normal University, the University of Yangzhou, Jiangsu Polytechnic University, Nanjing University of Technology, Xuzhou Normal University, Jiangsu Petrochemical College, Nanjing, Nanjing Auditing College School of Economics

ZHEJIANG

Zhejiang University, Zhejiang University, Ningbo University, Zhejiang Institute of Finance and Economics, Hangzhou University, Zhejiang University, Hangzhou Teachers College

ANHUI

China University of Science and Technology, Anhui University, Anhui Normal University, East China Institute of Metallurgy,

Anhui Institute of Finance and Trade, Huaibei Coal Teachers College, Hefei University of Technology

Fujian

Xiamen University, Fuzhou University, Chinese University, Fujian Normal University

Jiangxi

Nanchang University, Jiangxi Normal University, Jiangxi University of Finance and Economics, South Metallurgical Institute

Shandong

Shandong University, Ocean University of Qingdao, Shandong Normal University, the University of Yantai, Qingdao University, Shandong Engineering College, Shandong University, Jinan University, Shandong Institute of Financial

Henan

Henan University and Zhengzhou University, College of Engineering in Luoyang, Henan Institute of Finance and Economics and Management College in Zhengzhou Aviation Industry

Hubei

Wuhan University and Zhongnan University of Economics and Law, Huazhong University of Science and Technology, Hubei University, Wuhan University of Technology, the University of Huazhongshifan, China and South Africa Institute for Nationalities, Wuhan University of Science and Technology

HUNAN

Hunan University, Central South University, Hunan Normal University, the University of Xiangtan in Nanlin College, Changsha Institute of Traffic, Teachers College, Changde, Hunan Agricultural University

GUANGDONG

Sun Yat-sen University, Jinan University, South China University of Technology, South China Normal University and Shantou University, Shenzhen University, Guangdong University of Foreign Studies, Guangdong Business School

GUANGXI

Guangxi University, Guangxi Normal University

HAINAN

Hainan University

CHONGQING

Chongqing University and Southwest China Normal University, Southwest University of Political Science, Sichuan Foreign Language Institute, the Chongqing Business School, Southwest Petroleum Institute

SICHUAN

Sichuan University, the University of Electronic Science and Technology, Southwest Jiaotong University, Southwest University of Finance and Economics, Sichuan Normal University,

Southwest China Institute for Nationalities, Chengdu University of Technology, Sichuan Chemical Industry Institute of Light, Southwest University of Science and Technology, Sichuan Normal University

Guizhou

Guizhou University, Guizhou Institute for Nationalities, Guizhou University of Technology, Guizhou Normal University, Guizhou Financial Services Institute

Yunnan

Yunnan University, Kunming Polytechnic University, the Yunnan Institute for Nationalities

Tibet

Tibet Institute for Nationalities

Shaanxi

Northwest University, Xi'an Jiaotong University, Xi'an University of Technology, Shaanxi Normal University and Xi'an University of Science and Technology Building, Northwest Agricultural University of Science and Technology, the Northwest Institute of Political Science and Law, Northwestern University, Chang'an University, Shaanxi Economic Institute

Gansu

Lanzhou University, Northwest Normal University, Gansu Industrial University, the Northwest Institute for Nationalities, Maryland School of Business, Politics and Law Institute in Gansu

QINGHAI

National Institute of Qinghai Province, Qinghai Normal University

NINGXIA

Second Northwest Institute for Nationalities

XINJIANG

Xinjiang University, the Xinjiang Institute of Finance and Economics

Appendix B

Chinese Terms

Chinese	Pinyin	English Definition
北大法宝	bei da fa bao	A Chinese subscription legal-database service, akin to Westlaw and LexisNexis in the United States
打官司就是打关系	da guan si jiu shi da guan xi	In law, it's not what you know, it's who you know.
二奶村	er nai cun	Literally, "second-wife village," a phenomenon that describes a real-estate development or subdivision inhabited predominately by rich businessmen's mistresses
法	fa	Method, principle, or flow
法律	fa lü	Law
父母官	fu mu guan	Parental officials
公检法	gong jian fa	The judges, prosecutors, police, and all other actors on the governmental side of prosecution
工头	gong tou	Work head
官	guan	Official
关系	guan xi	Connection or relationship
律师	lü shi	Lawyer
老百姓	lao bai xing	Literally, "old hundred surnames," which means "all people"

(continued on next page)

Chinese	Pinyin	English Definition
户口	hu kou	The household registration system that China and many other countries use to officially identify a person as a resident of an area; it includes identifying information such as the name of the person, his date of birth, the names of his parents, and the name of his spouse, if married.
刊号	kan hao	Government-issued number that uniquely identifies a periodical
律	lü	Regulated
人怕官官怕洋	ren pa guan, guan pa yang	The people fear officials, the officials fear foreigners.
司法考试	si fa kao shi	Unified judicial examination
讼棍	song gun	Litigation tricksters
外夷	wai yi	Outer barbarians
中国	zhong guo	Middle Kingdom or China
信访局	xin fang jü	Bureau of Letters and Calls
人事档案	renshi dangan	Personnel file
存档机构	cundang jigou	Local labor agency

Appendix C
Sample Interview Questions

- Ideals
  - What motivated you to become a lawyer? What about lawyers in general?
  - How many lawyers did you know growing up?
  - What did you think being a lawyer would be like?
  - Why do so many people now want to be lawyers?
- Qualifications
  - Legal Education
    - Where did you receive your legal education?
    - What were your professors' backgrounds?
    - What was the curriculum like?
      - Is this curriculum uniform throughout the country?
      - Did you specialize in a certain field?
      - The degree you earned, what was it called?
      - Did you have to write a thesis?
    - Were there too many or too few seats in the legal-education program?
    - Are the funding opportunities adequate?
    - Did you go on internships? Where? When?
    - What was your legal library like?
      - What sources did it contain?
      - Was there an electronic database?
  - The Bar Exam
    - When did you take the bar?
    - How many times can you take it? What were the fees associated with it?

- What was the passage rate like the year you took the exam?
- How do you find out whether you passed?
- How have things changed since the introduction of the 司法考试?
  - Choosing a Job
    - Did you have a previous career choice?
    - How is the Chinese legal market right now?
    - What were your options?
    - What are the best jobs?
    - How do you get the best jobs?
      - Is the bar exam score important?
      - Are grades in college important?
      - What about *guanxi*?
    - Which jobs did you hold?
    - What was your practice field?
      - Were you able to choose your practice field?
      - Why did you choose this practice field?
  - Continuing Legal Education
    - Is continuing legal education available?
- Life as a Chinese Lawyer
  - Hierarchy
    - Who are your superiors? Inferiors?
    - Do you often interact with them?
    - Is there a generational difference between younger and older cohorts? What would that generational difference be?
  - What are the hours like?
  - What is billing like?
    - This billing method motivates you to take which types of cases? Reject which types of cases?
  - Your firm takes which types of clients—individuals or corporations?
  - How do you succeed as a Chinese lawyer?
    - Knowing the law?
    - Knowing the judge?

Sample Interview Questions

- - Party membership?
  - *Guanxi*? How do you build *guanxi*?
  ○ How do lawyers and judges salaries compare?
  ○ Judges
    - Do you interact with judges? When?
    - What is the quality and education of judges? What problems does this create?
    - Is there respect in the courtroom?
    - How is the reliability of the court system?
    - How do judges issue opinions? How long are the opinions?
  ○ How easy is it to move laterally into other firms? Other industries?
  ○ The privatization of the entire industry—what are the implications?
  ○ What are the biggest flaws of the Chinese law?
    - Procedural defects?
  ○ What is the rationale for the requirement to relinquish your license if you work for the government or a foreign firm?
- Personal Challenges (overlaps with the above)
  ○ What is the most satisfying part of your job? Least satisfying?
  ○ What are the biggest barriers; what do you find most frustrating?
- Practice Area Challenges
  ○ Do you specialize in a particular set of laws?
  ○ Do you handle many practice areas?
- Challenges of Chinese Lawyers as a Group
  ○ Where do you go to vent? Bars?
  ○ What is the public image of Chinese lawyers?
  ○ Do you belong to a bar?
  ○ How much unity is there in the bar?
  ○ How could unity be enhanced?
  ○ What is the biggest problem for the bar?
  ○ Do most of your colleagues perceive the bar as a potential political force?

- ○ What do you think about the ACLA? Does it adequately represent the interests of the bar?
- LLM-Specific Questions
  - ○ Why did you decide to apply for an LLM?
  - ○ How did you apply?
  - ○ How did you pay for this degree?
  - ○ What can this degree do for you when you return to China?
  - ○ Are you trying to pursue a JD? How does that advance your career?
- What are some good BBS sites or online forums where lawyers can freely express their opinions?

NOTES

INTRODUCTION

1. Ariana Eunjung Cha, "Protest Application Brings Labor Camp Threat, Woman Says," *Washington Post*, August 21, 2008.
2. Austin Ramzy, "Would-Be Beijing Protesters Punished," *Time Magazine*, August 21, 2008.
3. Ibid.
4. Max Weber, *Confucianisme et Taoøsme* (Paris: Gallimard, 2001), 215.
5. Ethan Michelson, "Unhooking from the State: Chinese Lawyers in Transition" (PhD diss., University of Chicago, 2002).
6. William Alford, "Of Lawyers Lost and Found: Searching for Legal Professionalism in the PRC," in *Raising the Bar: The Emerging Legal Profession in East Asia*, ed. William Alford (Cambridge, MA: Harvard University Press, 2007); and William Alford, *To Steal a Book Is an Elegant Offense: Intellectual Property Law in Chinese Civilization* (Stanford, CA: Stanford University Press, 1997).
7. Randall Peerenboom, "Let One Hundred Flowers Bloom, One Hundred Schools Contend: Debating Rule of Law in China," *Michigan Journal of International Law* 23 (2002).
8. Yves Dezalay and Bryant G. Garth, *Dealing in Virtue: International Commercial Arbitration and the Construction of a Transnational Legal Order* (Chicago: University of Chicago Press, 1996), 258.
9. Minxin Pei, "Political Changes in Post-Mao China: Progress and Challenges," in *China's Future: Constructive Partner or Emerging Threat?* ed. Ted Galen Carpenter and James A. Dorn, 301–305 (Washington, DC: Cato Institute, 2000).

CHAPTER 1

1. Oliver Wendell Holmes Jr., "The Path of the Law," *Harvard Law Review* 10 (1897): 457.
2. William Alford, "A Second Great Wall?: China's Post-Cultural Revolution Project of Legal Construction," *Cultural Dynamics* 11 (1999): 203.
3. *Caijing*, "Faces to Watch," *2008: Forecasts and Strategies* (2008): 48.

4. Shanghai municipal government, *2008 Shanghai Civil Service Recruitment Regulations.*

Chapter 2

1. This name was first recorded during the Warring States Period in *Shang Shu.*
2. Fuwei Shen, *Cultural Flow between China and Outside World throughout History* (Beijing: Foreign Languages Press, 1997), 33.
3. Annping Chin, *The Authentic Confucius: A Life of Thought and Politics* (New York: Scribner, 2007), 2.
4. Confucius, *The Analects of Confucius* (Whitefish: Kessinger Publishing, 2004), 87.
5. See, generally, James Legge, *The Chinese Classics* (London: Trübner and Co., 1869).
6. Frederick W. Mote, *Imperial China 900–1800* (Cambridge, MA: Harvard University Press, 2000), 126–135.
7. Ibid., 130.
8. T'ung-tsu Ch'u, "The Gentry and Local Administration in Ch'ing China," in *The Making of China: Main Themes in Premodern Chinese History*, ed. Chun-shu Chang, 313 (Englewood Cliffs, NJ: Prentice-Hall, 1975).
9. Pingti Ho, "Social Composition of Ming-Ch'ing Ruling Class," in *The Making of China: Main Themes in Premodern Chinese History*, ed. Chun-shu Chang, 298–309 (Englewood Cliffs, NJ: Prentice-Hall, 1975).
10. Mote, *Imperial China 900–1800*, 966.
11. Ibid., 636.
12. J. Mason Gentzler, *Changing China: Readings in the History of China from the Opium War to Present* (New York: Prager Publishers, 1977), 174.
13. Nathaniel Peffer, *China: The Collapse of a Civilization* (New York: The John Day Co., 1930), 19–20.
14. Ibid., 24.
15. Alford, *To Steal a Book Is an Elegant Offense*, 10–12.
16. Ibid., 12.
17. Peffer, *China: The Collapse of a Civilization*, 22.
18. Qiang Fang, "Were Chinese Rulers above the Law? Toward a Theory of the Rule of Law in China from Early Times to 1949 CE," *Stanford Journal of International Law* 44 (2008): 145.
19. William T. De Bary, *Sources of Chinese Tradition (New York: Columbia University Press, 1999),* 326.

20. Jonathan Spence, *To Change China: Western Advisors in China* (New York: Penguin Books, 1969), 32.
21. Shen, *Cultural Flow between China and Outside World*, 41.
22. Ibid., 21–41.
23. Mote, *Imperial China 900–1800*, 376–379.
24. See, generally, Spence, *To Change China: Western Advisors in China*.
25. Mote, *Imperial China 900–1800*, 953.
26. Ibid., 960.
27. Alford, *To Steal a Book Is an Elegant Offense*, 31.
28. For a more nuanced account, see John K. Fairbank, *The Chinese World Order: Traditional China's Foreign Relations* (Cambridge, MA: Harvard University Press, 1968).
29. Mote, *Imperial China 900–1800*, 961.
30. E. T. Backhouse, *Annals and Memoirs of the Court of Peking* (Boston: Houghton Mifflin, 1914), 325.
31. Frank Sanello, *Opium Wars: The Addiction of One Empire and the Corruption of Another* (Chicago: Sourcebooks, 2004), 39.
32. Ibid., 57–71.
33. See, generally, John K. Fairbank, *Trade and Diplomacy on the China Coast: The Opening of Treaty Ports, 1842–1854* (Stanford, CA: Stanford University Press, 1969).
34. See, generally, Melissa McCauley, *Social Power and Legal Culture: Litigation Masters in Late Imperial China* (Stanford, CA: Stanford University Press, 1999).
35. Derk Bodde, *Law in Imperial China* (Philadelphia: University of Pennsylvania Press, 1967), 415–417.
36. *Ci Hai*, abridged ed. (Shanghai: Shanghai Cishu Chubanshe, 1989), 903.
37. Deborah Cao, *Chinese Law: A Language Perspective* (Farnham, UK: Ashgate Publishing, 2004), 32.
38. McCauley, *Social Power and Legal Culture*, 10.
39. Weifang He, "China's Legal Profession: The Nascence and Growing Pains of a Professionalized Legal Class," *Columbia Journal of Asian Law* 19 (2005): 144.
40. Jonathan Spence, *Mao Zedong: A Penguin Life* (New York: Penguin Books, 1999), 12.
41. Jonathan Spence, *The Search for Modern China* (New York: W. W. Norton and Co., 1991), 264.
42. Gentzler, *Changing China*, 173.

43. Alison W. Conner, "To Get Rich Is Precarious: Regulation of Private Enterprise in the People's Republic of China," *Journal of Chinese Law* 5 (1991): 1.
44. Michelson, *Unhooking from the State*, 19.
45. Ibid.
46. Communist Party of China Central Committee, *Common Program of the China People's Consultative Congress* (Beijing: People's Press, 1982), sec. 17(21).
47. Michelson, *Unhooking from the State*, 97.
48. Ibid.
49. Gentzler, *Changing China*, 338.
50. Margaret MacMillan, *Nixon in China: The Week that Changed the World* (New York: Random House, 2008), 328.
51. Michelson, *Unhooking from the State*, 86.
52. Jerome Cohen, "Reforming China's Civil Procedure: Judging the Courts," *American Journal of Comparative Law* 45 (1997): 795.
53. NPC, *Provisional Regulations of the People's Republic of China on Lawyers*, sec. 1, http://www.chinalawinfo.com.
54. Xichuan Du and Lingyuan Zhang, *China's Legal System: A General Survey* (Beijing: New World Press, 1990), 195.
55. Michelson, *Unhooking from the State*, 86.
56. Ibid., 98.
57. Compare with the Soviet privatization experience in Pamela Jordan, *Defending Rights in Russia: Lawyers, the State, and Legal Reform in the Post-Soviet Era* (Vancouver: UBC Press, 2006).
58. Michelson, *Unhooking from the State*, 29.
59. Timothy Gelatt, "Lawyers in China: The Past Decade and Beyond," *New York Journal of International Law and Policy* 23 (1991): 753.
60. Michelson, *Unhooking from the State*, 63.
61. Ibid.
62. ACLA, "Brief Introduction," http://www.chineselawyer.com.cn/html/union/englishunion/briefintroduction.html.
63. Gelatt, *Lawyers in China*, 758.
64. Ibid., 789.
65. Michelson, *Unhooking from the State*, 64.
66. William Alford, "Tasselled Loafers for Barefoot Lawyers: Transformation and Tension in the World of Chinese Legal Workers," *China Quarterly* 141 (1995): 22–38.
67. Michelson, *Unhooking from the State*, 65.

68. Chengguang Wang and Qicai Gao, "Lushi Zhiye de Xianzhuang Diaocha: Wuhan Lushi Fangtian Zongshu [A Survey on the Current State of the Legal Profession: A Summary of Interviews from Wuhan]," *Chinese Lawyer Magazine* (December 5, 2000): 5–13.
69. NPC, *Provisional Regulations of the People's Republic of China on Lawyers*, http://www.chinalawinfo.com.
70. Michelson, *Unhooking from the State*, 46.
71. Ibid., 24.
72. Ibid., 67.
73. Lawyer interview 819, June 14, 2008.
74. Michelson, *Unhooking from the State*, 268.
75. NPC, *The Judges Law of the People's Republic of China*, http://www.chinalawinfo.com.
76. Ibid., sec. 4(9)(4).
77. Ibid., sec. 5.
78. Ibid., sec. 4(22).
79. NPC, *Lawyers Law of the People's Republic of China*, sec. 2(6).
80. Ibid., sec. 4.
81. Pan Wei, "Toward a Consultative Rule of Law Regime in China," in *Debating Political Reform in China: Rule of Law vs. Democratization*, 3 (New York: M. E. Sharpe, 2006).
82. *Chinese Lawyer Magazine*, "Progress in Improving the Functions of the Lawyers Association," May 1999.
83. Michelson, *Unhooking from the State*, 66.
84. Ibid., 257.
85. NPC, *Law of the People's Republic of China on Lawyers*, http://www.chinalawinfo.com.
86. Conner, *To Get Rich Is Precarious*.
87. World Bank World Development Indicators, "Real Historical GDP and Growth Rates," http://www.xici.net/b578140/d36370891.htm (accessed May 13, 2008).

Chapter 3

1. Roderick A. Macdonald, "Beyond Common Knowledge: Empirical Approaches to the Rule of Law," *Canadian Journal of Law and Society* 20.1 (2005): 211–213.

2. Thomas Carothers, "The Rule of Law Revival," *Foreign Affairs* (March 1998).
3. Eric W. Orts, "The Rule of Law in China," *Vanderbilt Journal of Transnational Law* 34 (2001): 74.
4. "Democracy," Dictionary.com Unabridged (version 1.1), http://www.dictionary.reference.com/browse/democracy (accessed April 2, 2008).
5. See, generally, Alexander Hamilton, *The Federalist Papers* (London: Penguin, 1987).
6. Brian Z. Tamanaha, *On the Rule of Law: History, Politics, Theory* (Cambridge: Cambridge University Press, 2004), 38.
7. Baron de Montesquieu, *The Spirit of Laws*, vol. 1 (New York: The Colonial Press, 1900), 150.
8. Randall Peerenboom, *Asian Discourses of Rule of Law* (New York: Routledge, 2004), 13.
9. See, generally, Thomas Carothers, *Promoting the Rule of Law Abroad: In Search of Knowledge* (Washington, DC: Carnegie Endowment for International Peace, 2006).
10. Franz Neumann, *The Rule of Law: Political Theory and the Legal System in Modern Society* (Oxford: Berg Publishing, 1986), 77–172.
11. Tamanaha, *On the Rule of Law*, 91–101.
12. Bryan A. Garner, "Prospective," *Black's Law Dictionary*, 8th ed. (2004).
13. Tamanaha, *On the Rule of Law*, 96.
14. Ibid.
15. Friedrich Hayek, *The Road to Serfdom: Texts and Documents* (Chicago: University of Chicago, 2007), 112.
16. T. R. S. Allan, *Constitutional Justice: A Liberal Theory of the Rule of Law* (Oxford: Oxford University Press, 2003), 2.
17. Tamanaha, *On the Rule of Law*, 123.
18. Ibid., 44.
19. Ibid., 123.
20. Alford, "Of Lawyers Lost and Found," 299.
21. Orts, "The Rule of Law in China," 101–102.
22. E. P. Thompson, *Whigs and Hunters: The Origin of the Black Acts* (New York: Pantheon Books, 1975), 266.
23. See, generally, Elaine Jeffreys, *China, Sex, and Prostitution* (London: Routledge, 2004).
24. Howard French, "Letter from China: The Sex Industry Is Everywhere but Nowhere," *International Herald Tribune*, December 14, 2006.

25. NPC, *The Marriage Law of the People's Republic of China*, http://www.chinalawinfo.com.
26. Shui Nuan Yun Dan, "Suffering Mistresses," *China Business News Network*, December 16, 2008.
27. *Caijing*, "Corruption Case of the Decade," *2008: Forecasts and Strategies* (2008): 30.
28. *China Daily*, "China Labor Act," July 6, 1994.
29. David Barboza, "Child Labor Cases Uncovered in China," *International Herald Tribune*, April 30, 2008.
30. *Southern Metropolis*, "Child Labor Black Market: Lack of Rule of Law Industry Decline," April 29, 2008.
31. Barboza, "Child Labor Cases Uncovered in China."
32. Working Party on Environmental Performance, "Environmental Performance Review of China" (Organisation for Economic Co-operation and Development, November 2006).
33. Ibid.
34. NPC, *The Product Quality Law of the People's Republic of China*, http://www.chinalawinfo.com.
35. NPC, *The Food Hygiene Law of the People's Republic of China*, http://www.chinalawinfo.com.
36. NPC, *The Product Quality Law of the People's Republic of China*, sec. 3(1)(28).
37. Ibid., sec. 2(8).
38. Ibid., sec. 1(15).
39. *Business Week*, "Wu Yi: China's Enforcer of Last Resort," September 24, 2007.
40. Mike Leavitt, "Statement by Secretary Mike Leavitt, Secretary of Health and Human Services, On Signing Memoranda of Agreement between the United States and The People's Republic of China to Improve the Safety of Food, Feed, Drugs and Medical Devices," U.S. Department of Health and Human Services, Washington, DC, December 11, 2007.
41. Ben Blanchard, "China Says Product Safety Push a Complete Success," Reuters, January 14, 2008.
42. Eijiro Ueno, "China Pesticide-Tainted Dumplings Poison 175 Japanese," Bloomberg, February 1, 2008.
43. Associated Press, "Insecticide Found on Dumplings in Japan," February 3, 2008.

44. PBS, "FDA Links Heparin Deaths to Contaminated Chinese Supply," *The Online NewsHour*, April 22, 2008, http://www.pbs.org/newshour/updates/health/jan-june08/heparin_04-22.html (accessed February 19, 2009).
45. Edward Wong, "Chinese Officials Say Tests Clear Formula Company," *New York Times*, February 16, 2009.
46. Associated Press, "12 More Arrested in China's Milk Case," *New York Times*, September 18, 2008.
47. Associated Press, "French Itch with Complaints over Chinese Chairs," MSNBC, September 19, 2008.
48. See, generally, Alford, *To Steal a Book Is an Elegant Offense*.
49. NPC, *The Trademark Law of the People's Republic of China* (1982).
50. NPC, *The Patent Law of the People's Republic of China* (1984).
51. See, generally, Alford, *To Steal a Book Is an Elegant Offense*.
52. Screen shots captured in September 2008.
53. Richard Owen, "Chinese Choccies Inflame Italian Passions," *The Times Online*, http://business.timesonline.co.uk/tol/business/law/corporate_law/article1290433.ece (accessed January 8, 2007).
54. Lawyer interview 324, June 26, 2008.
55. United States Trade Representative, "Special 301 Report," 2007.
56. United States Trade Representative, "Special 301 Report," 2008.
57. United States Trade Representative, "Special 301 Report," 2007.
58. Ibid.
59. ACCC, "2006 White Paper," 34.
60. ACCC, "2007 White Paper," 39.
61. ACCC, "2008 White Paper," 134.
62. Wei, "Toward a Consultative Rule of Law Regime in China," 3.
63. BBC, "China Admits Mismanaged Funds," August 28, 2008.
64. *Caijing*, "Corruption Case of the Decade." *2008: Forecasts and Strategies*, 2008.
65. Ibid., 28–29.
66. Matthew Philips, "China Regulates Buddhist Reincarnation," *Newsweek*, August 20, 2007.
67. Hayek, *The Road to Serfdom*, 112.
68. Yikun Zhu, *Concise Chinese Law* (Beijing: Legal Press, 2003), 11.
69. NPC, *The Judges Law of the People's Republic of China*, sec. 2(6), http://www.chinalawinfo.com.
70. Andrew Mertha, *The Politics of Piracy: Intellectual Property in Contemporary China* (Ithaca, NY: Cornell University Press, 2005), 222.
71. Ibid., 221.

72. Trade Lawyers Advisory Group, "The Crisis in Protecting Intellectual Property Rights" (United States–China Economic and Security Review Commission, May 2007), 115–117.
73. Lawyer interview 137, November 12, 2007.
74. Lawyer interview 675, January 1, 2008.
75. *Southern Metropolis*, "Child Labor Black Market."
76. Robert D. Cooter and Tom Ginsburg, "Leximetrics: Why the Same Laws Are Longer in Some Countries than Others" (research paper, University of Illinois Law and Economics, no. LE03-012, June 2003).
77. Ibid., 12.
78. John Wilson Lewis, *Major Doctrines of Communist China* (New York: W. W. Norton and Co., 1964), 11–51.
79. Zhu, *Concise Chinese Law*, 6.
80. NPC, Constitution of the People's Republic of China (1954).
81. NPC, Constitution of the People's Republic of China (1975).
82. NPC, Constitution of the People's Republic of China (1978).
83. NPC, Constitution of the People's Republic of China (1982).
84. See, generally, Macmillan, *Nixon in China*.
85. NPC, *The Trademark Law of the People's Republic of China* (1982).
86. NPC, *The Trademark Law of the People's Republic of China* (1993).
87. NPC, *The Trademark Law of the People's Republic of China* (2001).
88. NPC, *The Patent Law of the People's Republic of China* (1984).
89. NPC, *The Patent Law of the People's Republic of China* (1992).
90. NPC, *The Patent Law of the People's Republic of China* (2008).
91. Raymond Wacks, *Law: A Very Short Introduction* (Oxford: Oxford University Press, 2008), 21.
92. Trevor J. Saunders, *Politics* (London: Penguin Books, 1981).
93. Desmond Lee, *The Republic* (London: Penguin Classics, 1955).
94. See, generally, Frits Kern, *Kinship and Law in the Middle Ages* (New York: Harper Torch Books, 1956).
95. See, generally, Hugh Collins, *Marxism and Law* (Oxford: Oxford University Press, 1996).
96. See, generally, Thomas Blount, *Ancient Tenures*, 2nd ed. (1784 [out of print]).
97. Richard Pipes, *Property and Freedom* (New York: Vintage, 2000), 121–159.
98. See, generally, Henri Pirenne, *Economic and Social History of Medieval Europe* (Fort Washington, PA: Harvest Books, 1956).
99. Tamanaha, *On the Rule of Law*, 30.
100. Ibid., 141.

101. It must be noted that this account is weighted toward the history of Britain. Different parameters were present in France, Germany, and Italy.
102. Bo Wang, "Sex, Lies, and Videos in Rural China: A Qualitative Study of Women's Sexual Debut and Risky Sexual Behavior," *Journal of Sex Research* 43, no. 3 (2006): 227.
103. Allen T. Cheng, "China Has 106 Billionaires, Up From 15 Last Year," Bloomberg, October 10, 2007; *China Daily*, "China Has 146 Billionaires," January 1, 2008.
104. Elisabeth Rosenthal, "North of Beijing, California Dreams Come True," *New York Times*, February 3, 2003.
105. Richard Komaiko, "Wealthy Sovereign, Poor Citizen," *Asia Times*, February 14, 2008.
106. John Joseph, "Record $500,000 Paid for 27 Bottles of Red Wine," Reuters, April 19, 2008.
107. See, generally, Scott Kennedy, *The Business of Lobbying in China* (Cambridge, MA: Harvard University Press, 2005).
108. See, generally, Murray Scott Tanner, *The Politics of Lawmaking in Post-Mao China* (Oxford: Oxford University Press, 1999).
109. Zhisui Li, *The Private Life of Chairman Mao* (New York: Random House, 1996), 392.
110. Yangtze Yan, "Hu Jintao Mentions 'Democracy' More Than 60 Times in Landmark Report," Xinhua, October 15, 2007.
111. Robert Lawrence Kuhn, "Building Intra-Party Democracy in China," *Business Week*, February 20, 2008.
112. Paul Gewirtz, "The U.S.-China Rule of Law Initiative," *William & Mary Bill of Rights Journal* 11 (2003): 609.
113. Ibid.
114. Jamie Horsley, "The Rule of Law in China: Incremental Progress" (paper, China Balance Sheet in 2007 and Beyond Conference, Washington, DC, May 2, 2007), 2.
115. Xinhua, "White Paper: China's Efforts and Achievements in Promoting the Rule of Law," Information Office of the State Council of PRC, February 28, 2008, http://news.xinhuanet.com/english/2008-02/28/content_7687418.htm.
116. Tamanaha, *On the Rule of Law*, 141.

Chapter 4

1. Lawyer interview 354, April 21, 2008.
2. Lawyer interview 845, April 21, 2008.

3. Lawyer interview 238, April 28, 2008.
4. Lawyer interview 766, April 25, 2008.
5. Lawyer interview 712, June 29, 2008.
6. Lawyer interview 783, April 23, 2008.
7. Lawyer interview 824, April 27, 2008.
8. Lawyer interview 712, June 29, 2008.
9. Chen, "What Is the Difference between Lawyers and Businessmen."
10. Sina Education, "2007 Chinese Universities A List Law Programs."
11. Lawyer interview 936, April 27, 2008.
12. Ibid.
13. Lawyer interview 693, April 21, 2008.
14. Ibid.
15. Lawyer interview 796, April 23, 2008.
16. Lawyer interview 463, April 8, 2008.
17. Lawyer interview 693, April 21, 2008.
18. NPC, *Law of the People's Republic of China on Lawyers*, http://www.chinalawinfo.com.
19. NPC, *The Judges Law of the People's Republic of China*, http://www.chinalawinfo.com.

CHAPTER 5

1. Xuecun Murong, *Dancing through Red Dust* (Zhuhai: Zhuhai Chubanshe, 2008).
2. Cf. Katherine Xin and Jone Pearce, "Guanxi: Connections as Substitutes for Formal Institutional Support," *Academy of Management Journal* 39, no. 6 (1996).
3. Tahirih V. Lee, *Contract, Guanxi, and Dispute Resolution in China* (New York: Routledge, 1997).
4. Lawyer interview 902, May 15, 2008.
5. Lawyer interview 192, April 3, 2008.
6. Lawyer interview 715, April 4, 2008.
7. Lawyer interview 908, May 5, 2008.
8. Lawyer interview 458, June 18, 2008.
9. Lawyer interview 870, February 8, 2008.
10. Lawyer interview 904, July 17, 2008.
11. Lawyer interview 613, June 13, 2008.
12. Lawyer interview 604, August 10, 2008.
13. Lawyer interview 464, June 3, 2008.

14. Lawyer interview 254, April 18, 2008.
15. Lawyer interview 147, April 29, 2008.
16. Lawyer interview 366, June 4, 2008.
17. Lawyer interview 805, May 27, 2008.
18. Lawyer interview 667, June 18, 2008.
19. Lawyer interview 629, April 11, 2008.
20. Lawyer interview 324, June 26, 2008.
21. Lawyer interview 580, April 21, 2008.

Chapter 6

1. Lawyer interview 248, June 8, 2008.
2. See, generally, Young Lawyers Committee, "Investigation Into the Life of Young Lawyers—青年律师生存状态调查" (Shanghai Bar Association, 2006).
3. Lawyer interview 354, April 21, 2008.
4. Lawyer interview 783, April 23, 2008.
5. Lawyer interview 458, June 18, 2008.
6. Lawyer interview 678, April 21, 2008.
7. Jennifer Smith and Michael Gompers, "Realizing Justice: The Development of Fair Trial Rights in China," *Chinese Law and Policy Review* 2, no. 10 (2007): 27.
8. Lawyer interview 580, April 21, 2008.
9. Lawyer interview 152, December 16, 2007; lawyer interview 580, April 21, 2008.
10. Lawyer interview 147, April 29, 2008.
11. Lawyer interview with Zhang Guojun, June 27, 2008.
12. Ibid.
13. Lawyer interview 319, April 27, 2008.
14. Lawyer interview 436, June 26, 2008.
15. Douglas McCollam, "The Billable Hour: Are Its Days Numbered?" The American Lawyer, http://www.law.com/jsp/ihc/PubArticleIHC.jsp?id=1132653918886.
16. See also Nuno Garoupa and Fernando Gomez-Pomar, "Cashing by the Hour: Why Large Law Firms Prefer Hourly Fees over Contingent Fees," *Journal of Law, Economics and Organization* 24 (2008).
17. Alford, "Tasselled Loafers for Barefoot Lawyers," 195.

18. Lawyer interview 277, June 29, 2008.
19. See, generally, Xianzhang Liu, *Lawyer's Basic Professional Cultivation* (Beijing: Beijing University Press, 2007).
20. Lawyer interview 602, June 8, 2008.
21. Lawyer interview 463, April 8, 2008.
22. Young Lawyers Committee, *Investigation into the Life of Young Lawyers*.
23. Michelson, "Gender Inequality in the Chinese Legal Profession," *Research in the Sociology of Work* 18 (2009).
24. Lawyer interview 793, April 29, 2008.

Chapter 7

1. Lawyer interview 580, April 21, 2008.
2. Xinhua, "China's Lawyers Failing to Provide Nationwide Service," *People's Daily Online*, July 10, 2006.
3. Lawyer populations.
4. Smith and Gompers, *Realizing Justice*, 10.
5. Counties, "Divisions of Administrative Areas in China," China.org.
6. Fazhiwang, "China: 206 Counties Have No Lawyers—Access to Lawyers Is Increasingly Difficult for the Lower Class," CCTV, http://news.cctv.com/law/20061224/100536.shtml.
7. Sida Liu, "The Logic of Regulating Chinese Lawyers Fees," *Shanghai Lawyer Magazine* 1, 15.
8. Young Lawyers Committee, *Investigation into the Life of Young Lawyers*.
9. AFP, "Urban Chinese Employees' Average Salary Up 18.7%," *The China Post*, April 3, 2008.
10. Michelson, *Unhooking from the State*, 189–238.
11. Børge Bakken, *The Exemplary Society: Human Improvement, Social Control, and the Dangers of Modernity in China* (Oxford: Oxford University Press: 2000), 288–297.
12. Lawyer interview 719, January 23, 2008.
13. Lawyer interview 796, April 23, 2008.
14. Lawyer interview with Yu Zong, April 27, 2008.
15. Baidu Answers, "Urban Populations," http://zhidao.baidu.com/question/56406034.html.

Chapter 8

1. E. P. Thompson, *Whigs and Hunters: The Origin of the Black Acts* (New York: Pantheon Books, 1975), 266.
2. This number was the product of regression analysis with 95 percent confidence.

Conclusion

1. World Bank World Development Indicators, "Real Historical GDP and Growth Rates."
2. Sunita Kikero and Aishetu Kolo, "State Enterprises," World Bank—Public Policy for the Private Sector, note 34, 2006.
3. Cf. Fudan University School of Law, "Fudan University Student Enrollment Roster."

BIBLIOGRAPHY

AFP. "Urban Chinese Employees' Average Salary Up 18.7%." *The China Post*, April 3, 2008.

Alford, William. "Of Lawyers Lost and Found: Searching for Legal Professionalism in the PRC." In *Raising the Bar: The Emerging Legal Profession in East Asia*, edited by William Alford, 287–310. Cambridge, MA: Harvard University Press, 2007.

———. "A Second Great Wall?: China's Post-Cultural Revolution Project of Legal Construction." *Cultural Dynamics* 11 (1999): 193–213.

———. "Tasselled Loafers for Barefoot Lawyers: Transformation and Tension in the World of Chinese Legal Workers." *China Quarterly* 141 (1995): 22–38.

———. *To Steal a Book Is an Elegant Offense: Intellectual Property Law in Chinese Civilization*. Stanford, CA: Stanford University Press, 1997.

All China Lawyers Association (ACLA). "Brief Introduction." http://www.chineselawyer.com.cn/html/union/englishunion/briefintroduction.html.

Allan, T. R. S. *Constitutional Justice: A Liberal Theory of the Rule of Law*. Oxford: Oxford University Press, 2003.

American Bar Association Department of Market Research. "National Lawyer Population by State." http://www.abanet.org/marketresearch/2007_Natl_Lawyer_FINALonepage.pdf.

American Chamber of Commerce in China (ACCC). "2006 White Paper."

———. "2007 White Paper."

———. "2008 White Paper."

Associated Press. "12 More Arrested in China's Milk Case." *New York Times*, September 18, 2008.

———. "French Itch with Complaints over Chinese Chairs." MSNBC, September 19, 2008.

———. "Insecticide Found on Dumplings in Japan." February 3, 2008.

Backhouse, E. T. *Annals and Memoirs of the Court of Peking.* Boston: Houghton Mifflin, 1914.

Baidu Answers. "Urban Populations." http://zhidao.baidu.com/question/56406034.html.

Bakken, Børge. *The Exemplary Society: Human Improvement, Social Control, and the Dangers of Modernity in China.* Oxford: Oxford University Press, 2000.

Barboza, David. "Child Labor Cases Uncovered in China." *International Herald Tribune*, April 30, 2008.

BBC. "China Admits Mismanaged Funds." August 28, 2008.

Benetton, Luigi. "Few Law Firms in Canada are Outsourcing Legal Work to India." *The Lawyers Weekly*, November 27, 2007.

Blanchard, Ben. "China Says Product Safety Push a Complete Success." Reuters, January 14, 2008.

Blount, Thomas. *Ancient Tenures*. 2nd ed. 1784 [out of print].

Bodde, Derk. *Law in Imperial China.* Philadelphia: University of Pennsylvania Press, 1967.

Business Week. "Wu Yi: China's Enforcer of Last Resort." September 24, 2007.

Caijing. "Corruption Case of the Decade." *2008: Forecasts and Strategies.* 2008.

———. "A Talk with the Top Prosecutor." *2008: Forecasts and Strategies.*

Canlaw Database. http://www.canlaw.com/lawyers/membership.htm.

Cao, Deborah. *Chinese Law: A Language Perspective.* Farnham, UK: Ashgate Publishing, 2004.

Carothers, Thomas. *Promoting the Rule of Law Abroad: In Search of Knowledge.* Washington, DC: Carnegie Endowment for International Peace, 2006.

———. "The Rule of Law Revival." *Foreign Affairs* (March/April 1998).

Cha, Ariana Eunjung. "Protest Application Brings Labor Camp Threat, Woman Says." *Washington Post*, August 21, 2008.

Chen, Mo. "What Is the Difference between Lawyers and Businessmen." Guangzhou Department of Justice, October 10, 2007.

Cheng, Allen T. "China Has 106 Billionaires, Up From 15 Last Year." Bloomberg, October 10, 2007.

Chin, Annping. *The Authentic Confucius: A Life of Thought and Politics.* New York: Scribner, 2007.

China Daily. "China Has 146 Billionaires." January 1, 2008.

———. "China Labor Act." July 6, 1994.

Chinese Lawyer Magazine. "Progress in Improving the Functions of the Lawyers Association." May 1999.

Ch'u, T'ung-tsu. "The Gentry and Local Administration in Ch'ing China." In *The Making of China: Main Themes in Premodern Chinese History*, edited by Chun-shu Chang, 310–329. Englewood Cliffs, NJ: Prentice-Hall, 1975.

CIA World Factbook. https://www.cia.gov/library/publications/the-world-factbook.

Ci Hai. Abridged ed. Shanghai: Shanghai Cishu Chubanshe, 1989.

Cohen, Jerome. "Reforming China's Civil Procedure: Judging the Courts." *American Journal of Comparative Law* 45 (1997): 793–804.

Collins, Hugh. *Marxism and Law.* Oxford: Oxford University Press, 1996.

Communist Party of China Central Committee. *Common Program of the China People's Consultative Congress.* Beijing: People's Press, 1982.

Confucius. *The Analects of Confucius.* Whitefish: Kessinger Publishing, 2004.

Conner, Alison W. "To Get Rich Is Precarious: Regulation of Private Enterprise in the People's Republic of China." *Journal of Chinese Law* 5 (1991): 1–57.

———. "Training China's Early Modern Lawyers: Soochow University Law School." *Journal of Chinese Law* 8 (1994): 1–45.

Consumer Product Safety Commission. http://www.cpsc.gov/cgi-bin/cmfg.aspx.

Cooter, Robert D., and Tom Ginsburg. "Leximetrics: Why the Same Laws Are Longer in Some Countries than Others." Research paper, University of Illinois Law and Economics, no. LE03-012, June 2003.

Council of Bars and Law Societies of Europe (CCBE). "Number of Lawyers in CCBE Member Bars." www.ccbe.org/fileadmin/user_upload/NTCdocument/table_number_lawyers1_1179905628.pdf.

Counties. "Divisions of Administrative Areas in China." China.org.

De Bary, William T. *Sources of Chinese Tradition.* New York: Columbia University Press, 1999.

Dezalay, Yves, and Bryant G. Garth. *Dealing in Virtue: International Commercial Arbitration and the Construction of a Transnational Legal Order.* Chicago: University of Chicago Press, 1996.

Dictionary.com Unabridged (version 1.1). "Democracy." http://dictionary.reference.com/browse/democracy.

Du, Xichuan, and Lingyuan Zhang. *China's Legal System: A General Survey.* Beijing: New World Press, 1990.

Fairbank, John K. *The Chinese World Order: Traditional China's Foreign Relations.* Cambridge, MA: Harvard University Press, 1968.

———. *Trade and Diplomacy on the China Coast: The Opening of Treaty Ports, 1842–1854.* Stanford, CA: Stanford University Press, 1969.

Fang, Qiang. "Were Chinese Rulers above the Law? Toward a Theory of the Rule of Law in China from Early Times to 1949 CE." *Stanford Journal of International Law* 44 (2008): 101–146.

Fazhiwang. "China: 206 Counties Have No Lawyers—Access to Lawyers Is Increasingly Difficult for the Lower Class." CCTV. http://news.cctv.com/law/20061224/100536.shtml.

French, Howard. "Letter from China: The Sex Industry Is Everywhere but Nowhere." *International Herald Tribune*, December 14, 2006.

Fudan University School of Law. "Fudan University Student Enrollment Roster."

Garner, Bryan A. "Prospective." In *Black's Law Dictionary*, 8th ed. 2004.

Garoupa, Nuno, and Fernando Gomez-Pomar. "Cashing by the Hour: Why Large Law Firms Prefer Hourly Fees over Contingent Fees." *Journal of Law, Economics and Organization* 24 (2008): 458–475.

Gelatt, Timothy. "Lawyers in China: The Past Decade and Beyond." *New York Journal of International Law and Policy* 23 (1991): 751–801.

Gentzler, J. Mason. *Changing China: Readings in the History of China from the Opium War to Present.* New York: Prager Publishers, 1977.

Gewirtz, Paul. "The U.S.-China Rule of Law Initiative." *William & Mary Bill of Rights Journal* 11 (2003): 603–621.

Hamilton, Alexander. *The Federalist Papers.* London: Penguin, 1987.

Hayek, Friedrich. *The Road to Serfdom: Texts and Documents.* Chicago: University of Chicago Press, 2007.

He, Weifang. "China's Legal Profession: The Nascence and Growing Pains of a Professionalized Legal Class." *Columbia Journal of Asian Law* 19 (2005): 138–151.

Ho, Pingti. "Social Composition of Ming-Ch'ing Ruling Class." In *The Making of China: Main Themes in Premodern Chinese History*, edited by Chun-shu Chang, 298–309. Englewood Cliffs, NJ: Prentice-Hall, 1975.

Holmes, Oliver Wendell Jr. "The Path of the Law." *Harvard Law Review* 10 (1897): 457–478.

Horsley, Jamie. "The Rule of Law in China: Incremental Progress." Paper presented at the China Balance Sheet in 2007 and Beyond Conference, Washington, DC, May 2, 2007.

Jeffreys, Elaine. *China, Sex, and Prostitution*. London: Routledge, 2004.

Jordan, Pamela. *Defending Rights in Russia: Lawyers, the State, and Legal Reform in the Post-Soviet Era*. Vancouver: UBC Press, 2006.

Joseph, John. "Record $500,000 Paid for 27 Bottles of Red Wine." Reuters, April 19, 2008.

Kennedy, Scott. *The Business of Lobbying in China*. Cambridge, MA: Harvard University Press, 2005.

Kern, Frits. *Kinship and Law in the Middle Ages*. New York: Harper Torch Books, 1956.

Kikero, Sunita, and Aishetu Kolo. "State Enterprises." World Bank—Public Policy for the Private Sector, note 34, 2006.

Kircher, Athanasius. *China Monumentis qua Sacris qua Profanis*. Amsterdam: Apud Jacobum a Meurs, 1667.

Komaiko, Richard. "Wealthy Sovereign, Poor Citizen." *Asia Times*, February 14, 2008.

Kuhn, Robert Lawrence. "Building Intra-Party Democracy in China." *Business Week*, February 20, 2008.

Law Council of Australia. "LCA Brief—September 2004." http://www.lawcouncil.asn.au/shadomx/apps/fms/fmsdownload.cfm?file_uuid=8B6DE76E-1C23-CACD-220D-D598F65A739A&siteName=lca.

Lawyer interview 137, November 12, 2007.

Lawyer interview 147, April 29, 2008.

Lawyer interview 152, December 16, 2007.

Lawyer interview 192, April 3, 2008.

Lawyer interview 238, April 28, 2008.

Lawyer interview 248, June 8, 2008.

Lawyer interview 254, April 18, 2008.

Lawyer interview 277, June 29, 2008.

Lawyer interview 319, April 27, 2008.

Lawyer interview 324, June 26, 2008.

Lawyer interview 354, April 21, 2008.

Lawyer interview 366, June 4, 2008.

Lawyer interview 436, June 26, 2008.

Lawyer interview 458, June 18, 2008.

Lawyer interview 463, July 19, 2008.

Lawyer interview 464, June 3, 2008.

Lawyer interview 580, April 21, 2008.

Lawyer interview 602, June 8, 2008.

Lawyer interview 604, July 3, 2008.

Lawyer interview 613, June 13, 2008.

Lawyer interview 629, April 11, 2008.

Lawyer interview 667, June 18, 2008.

Lawyer interview 675, January 1, 2008.
Lawyer interview 678, April 21, 2008.
Lawyer interview 693, April 21, 2008.
Lawyer interview 712, June 29, 2008.
Lawyer interview 715, April 4, 2008.
Lawyer interview 719, January 23, 2008.
Lawyer interview 766, April 25, 2008.
Lawyer interview 783, April 23, 2008.
Lawyer interview 793, April 29, 2008.
Lawyer interview 796, April 23, 2008.
Lawyer interview 805, May 27, 2008.
Lawyer interview 819, June 12, 2008.
Lawyer interview 824, April 27, 2008.
Lawyer interview 845, April 21, 2008.
Lawyer interview 870, February 8, 2008.
Lawyer interview 902, May 15, 2008.
Lawyer interview 904, July 17, 2008.
Lawyer interview 908, May 5, 2008.
Lawyer interview 936, April 27, 2008.
Lawyer interview with Yu Zong, April 27, 2008.
Lawyer interview with Zhang Guojun, June 27, 2008.
Leavitt, Mike. "Statement by Secretary Mike Leavitt, Secretary of Health and Human Services, On Signing Memoranda of Agreement between the United States and the People's Republic of China to Improve the Safety of Food, Feed, Drugs and Medical Devices." U.S. Department of Health and Human Services, Washington, DC, December 11, 2007.

Bibliography

Lee, Desmond. *The Republic.* London: Penguin Classics, 1955.

Lee, Tahirih V. *Contract, Guanxi, and Dispute Resolution in China.* New York: Routledge, 1997.

Legge, James. *The Chinese Classics.* London: Trübner and Co., 1869.

Lewis, John Wilson. *Major Doctrines of Communist China.* New York: W. W. Norton and Co., 1964.

Li, Zhisui. *The Private Life of Chairman Mao.* New York: Random House, 1996.

Liu, Sida. "The Logic of Regulating Chinese Lawyers Fees." *Shanghai Lawyer Magazine*, 15.

Liu, Xianzhang. *Lawyer's Basic Professional Cultivation.* Beijing: Beijing University Press, 2007.

Macdonald, Roderick A. "Beyond Common Knowledge: Empirical Approaches to the Rule of Law." *Canadian Journal of Law and Society* 20, no. 1 (2005): 211–213.

Macmillan, Margaret. *Nixon in China: The Week that Changed the World.* New York: Random House, 2008.

McCauley, Melissa. *Social Power and Legal Culture: Litigation Masters in Late Imperial China.* Stanford, CA: Stanford University Press, 1999.

McCollam, Douglas. "The Billable Hour: Are Its Days Numbered?" The American Lawyer. http://www.law.com/jsp/ihc/PubArticleIHC.jsp?id=1132653918886.

Mertha, Andrew. *The Politics of Piracy: Intellectual Property in Contemporary China.* Ithaca, NY: Cornell University Press, 2005.

Michelson, Ethan. "Gender Inequality in the Chinese Legal Profession." *Research in the Sociology of Work* 18 (2009).

———. *Unhooking from the State: Chinese Lawyers in Transition.* PhD diss., University of Chicago, 2002.

Montesquieu, Baron de. *The Spirit of Laws*. Vol. 1. New York: The Colonial Press, 1900.

Mote, Frederick W. *Imperial China 900–1800*. Cambridge, MA: Harvard University Press, 2000.

Murong, Xuecun. *Dancing through Red Dust*. Zhuhai: Zhuhai Chubanshe, 2008.

Neumann, Franz. *The Rule of Law: Political Theory and the Legal System in Modern Society*. Oxford: Berg Publishing, 1986.

National People's Congress (NPC). Constitution of the People's Republic of China (1954).

———. Constitution of the People's Republic of China (1975).

———. Constitution of the People's Republic of China (1978).

———. Constitution of the People's Republic of China (1982).

———. *The Food Hygiene Law of the People's Republic of China* (October 30, 1995). http:///www.chinalawinfo.com.

———. *The Judges Law of the People's Republic of China* (January 1, 1995). http:///www.chinalawinfo.com.

———. *Law of the People's Republic of China on Lawyers* (October 28, 2007). http:///www.chinalawinfo.com.

———. *Lawyers Law of the People's Republic of China* (May 15, 1996). http:///www.chinalawinfo.com.

———. *The Marriage Law of the People's Republic of China* (April 28, 2001). http:///www.chinalawinfo.com.

———. *The Patent Law of the People's Republic of China* (March 12, 1984). http:///www.chinalawinfo.com.

———. *The Patent Law of the People's Republic of China* (September 4, 1992). http:///www.chinalawinfo.com.

———. *The Patent Law of the People's Republic of China* (December 27, 2008). http:///www.chinalawinfo.com.

———. *The Product Quality Law of the People's Republic of China* (July 8, 2000). http:///www.chinalawinfo.com.

———. *Provisional Regulations of the People's Republic of China on Lawyers* (August 27, 1980). http:///www.chinalawinfo.com.

———. *The Trademark Law of the People's Republic of China* (August 23, 1982). http:///www.chinalawinfo.com.

———. *The Trademark Law of the People's Republic of China* (February 22, 1993). http:///www.chinalawinfo.com.

———. *The Trademark Law of the People's Republic of China* (October 27, 2001). http:///www.chinalawinfo.com.

Ordem dos Advogados do Brasil. "Quadro de Advogados—Regulares e Recadastrados." http://www.oab.org.br/relatorioAdvOAB.asp.

Orts, Eric W. "The Rule of Law in China." *Vanderbilt Journal of Transnational Law* 34 (2001): 43–115.

Owen, Richard. "Chinese Choccies Inflame Italian Passions." *The Times Online*. http://business.timesonline.co.uk/tol/business/law/corporate_law/article1290433.ece.

PBS. "FDA Links Heparin Deaths to Contaminated Chinese Supply." *The Online NewsHour*, April 22, 2008. http://www.pbs.org/newshour/updates/health/jan-june08/heparin_04-22.html.

Peerenboom, Randall. *Asian Discourses of Rule of Law*. New York: Routledge, 2004.

———. "Let One Hundred Flowers Bloom, One Hundred Schools Contend: Debating Rule of Law in China." *Michigan Journal of International Law* 23 (2002): 471–544.

Peffer, Nathaniel. *China: The Collapse of a Civilization*. New York: The John Day Co., 1930.

Pei, Minxin. "Political Changes in Post-Mao China: Progress and Challenges." In *China's Future: Constructive Partner or Emerging Threat?*

edited by Ted Galen Carpenter and James A. Dorn, 291–316. Washington, DC: Cato Institute, 2000.

Philips, Matthew. "China Regulates Buddhist Reincarnation." *Newsweek*, August 20, 2007.

Pipes, Richard. *Property and Freedom.* New York: Vintage, 2000.

Pirenne, Henri. *Economic and Social History of Medieval Europe.* Fort Washington, PA: Harvest Books, 1956.

Ramzy, Austin. "Would-Be Beijing Protesters Punished." *Time Magazine*, August 21, 2008.

Rosenthal, Elisabeth. "North of Beijing, California Dreams Come True." *New York Times*, February 3, 2003.

Sanello, Frank. *The Opium Wars: The Addiction of One Empire and the Corruption of Another.* Chicago: Sourcebooks, 2004.

Saunders, Trevor J. *Politics.* London: Penguin Books, 1981.

Shen, Fuwei. *Cultural Flow between China and Outside World throughout History.* Beijing: Foreign Languages Press, 1997.

Sina Education. "2007 Chinese Universities A List Law Programs." http://edu.sina.com.cn/l/2007-01-08/1747136912.html.

———. "National Unified Judicial Examination High Passage Rate Opportunity." http://edu.sina.com.cn/zgks/2009-07-17/1047210617.shtml.

Smith, Jennifer, and Michael Gompers. "Realizing Justice: The Development of Fair Trial Rights in China." *Chinese Law & Policy Review* 2, no. 10 (2007): 108–140.

Southern Metropolis. "Child Labor Black Market: Lack of Rule of Law Industry Decline." April 29, 2008.

Spence, Jonathan. *Mao Zedong: A Penguin Life.* New York: Penguin Books, 1999.

———. *The Search for Modern China.* New York: W. W. Norton and Co., 1991.

———. *To Change China: Western Advisors in China.* New York: Penguin Books, 1969.

Tamanaha, Brian Z. *On the Rule of Law: History, Politics, Theory.* Cambridge: Cambridge University Press, 2004.

Tanner, Murray Scott. *The Politics of Lawmaking in Post-Mao China.* Oxford: Oxford University Press, 1999.

Thompson, E. P. *Whigs and Hunters: The Origin of the Black Acts.* New York: Pantheon Books, 1975.

Trade Lawyers Advisory Group. "The Crisis in Protecting Intellectual Property Rights." United States–China Economic and Security Review Commission, May 2007.

Ueno, Eijiro. "China Pesticide-Tainted Dumplings Poison 175 Japanese." Bloomberg, February 1, 2008.

United States Trade Representative. "Special 301 Report." 2007.

———. "Special 301 Report." 2008.

Wacks, Raymond. *Law: A Very Short Introduction.* Oxford: Oxford University Press, 2008.

Wang, Bo. "Sex, Lies, and Videos in Rural China: A Qualitative Study of Women's Sexual Debut and Risky Sexual Behavior." *Journal of Sex Research* 43, no. 3 (2006): 227–235.

Wang, Chengguang, and Qicai Gao. "Lushi Zhiye de Xianzhuang Diaocha: Wuhan Lushi Fangtian Zongshu [A Survey on the Current State of the Legal Profession: A Summary of Interviews from Wuhan]." *Chinese Lawyer Magazine* (December 5, 2000).

Weber, Max. *Confucianisme et Taoøsme.* Paris: Gallimard, 2001.

Wei, Pan. "Toward a Consultative Rule of Law Regime in China." In *Debating Political Reform in China: Rule of Law vs. Democratization*, 3–40. New York: M. E. Sharpe, 2006.

Wong, Edward. "Chinese Officials Say Tests Clear Formula Company." *New York Times*, February 16, 2009.

Working Party on Environmental Performance. "Environmental Performance Review of China." Organisation for Economic Co-operation and Development, November 2006.

World Bank World Development Indicators. "Real Historical GDP and Growth Rates." http://www.xici.net/b578140/d36370891.htm.

Xin, Katherine, and Jone Pearce. "Guanxi: Connections as Substitutes for Formal Institutional Support." *Academy of Management Journal* 39, no. 6 (1996): 1641–1658.

Xinhua. "China's Lawyers Failing to Provide Nationwide Service." *People's Daily Online*, July 10, 2006.

———. "White Paper: China's Efforts and Achievements in Promoting the Rule of Law." Information Office of the State Council of PRC. http://news.xinhuanet.com/english/2008-02/28/content_7687418.htm

Yan, Yangtze. "Hu Jintao Mentions 'Democracy' More Than 60 Times in Landmark Report." Xinhua, October 15, 2007.

Young Lawyers Committee. "Investigation into the Life of Young Lawyers—青年律师生存状态调查." Shanghai Bar Association, 2006.

Yun Dan, and Shui Nuan. "Suffering Mistresses." *China Business News Network*, December 16, 2008.

Zhu, Yikun. *Concise Chinese Law*. Beijing: Legal Press, 2003.

INDEX

Abraham Lincoln, 9, 94
Alford, William, 4, 12
All China Lawyers Assocation (ACLA), 41, 48–49, 105, 110, 176
Ally McBeal, 92, 109
American Chamber of Commerce in China (ACCC), 67–68
Andrew Mertha, 71
authority, heirarchy of, 4, 8, 17, 19, 25, 32, 45, 51, 56, 70–71, 115, 124, 141

barbarian, 16, 21, 24–25, 27, 29, 32
Beida fabao, 123, 157
Beijing, 1, 5, 26, 29, 32, 37, 39, 49, 61, 63, 65, 74, 87–88, 96, 118, 123, 130, 134–135, 137, 139, 143, 157
Beijing University, 96, 123, 157
billable hour, 127–129
Boston Legal, 92, 109

Caijing Magazine, 13
Cicero, Marcus Tullius, 80
civil service exam, 18
classics, the, 17–21, 23, 29, 32–33, 51, 81, 159–160
Communist Party, 4, 13, 33–36, 40, 59, 69, 76–79, 85–89, 107, 151
Congress, 13, 40, 88
Confucius, 16, 20–21, 33, 97
constitution, 33, 40–41, 75, 77–78, 89, 102, 118, 123
Cooter, Robert, 76

copyright law, 65, 67
counterfeit, 67–68, 72–73, 139
court, 7–11, 25, 37–39, 41, 43, 45–46, 71, 73–75, 82, 95, 97, 105–106, 111, 114, 116–117, 123–124, 158

Deng, Xiaoping, 12, 36, 41, 88
directory of lawyers, 143–144, 148, 156–157
DVD, 65, 98

emperor, 18–19, 21–22, 25, 27–30, 32–33

Facebook, 65–66
Fang Da Partners, 123
feudalism, 33, 81–85, 89
Food and Drug Administration (FDA), 64
food hygiene law, 62, 70
frustration, 1–3, 5, 121–126, 129, 158–159
Fudan University, 96–98, 101–102, 126
fumu guan, 20

gaokao, 92
gender equality, 130
George III, King of England, 22, 27
Ginsburg, Thomas, 76
gongjianfa, 38, 44
gross domestic product (GDP), 64, 135, 138
guanxi, 48, 110, 113

Hart, H. L. A., 3
Hebei Province, 64
Hu, Jintao, 12–13, 88
hukou, 144–147
Hundred Flowers Campaign, 35–36, 50

Japanese invasion, 34–35
Jiang, Jieshi, 34
Jiang, Zemin, 12–13
Jilin, 94, 96, 126
judges law, 45
justice, 7, 93, 97, 158

Law and Order, 92
law firm, 127, 141
   cooperative model, 42
   gong tou model, 142–143, 171
   partnership model, 42, 142
   state legal advisory office, 41
law review, 101, 113, 125–126, 156
lawyers law, 40, 46–47, 49
lawyers license, 43–44, 47, 49, 105–106, 135, 156
legal research, 102, 156–157
leximetrics, 75, 78
liability, 74, 76, 128, 153, 155
   culture of, 74, 128–129, 147, 152
   fear of, 128, 148
liberty, 54–56, 146
Lu Xun, 95
lüshi, 31

mandate of heaven, 21, 23, 29, 32, 51, 158–159, 161
Mao, Zedong, 12, 33, 34–36, 48, 76, 78, 81
market for legal services, 5, 30, 133–149

market for legal services (*continued*)
   obstacles to functioning, 143–148
   policies to improve, 152–156
Marx, Karl, 35, 48, 77, 81
Michelson, Ethan, 3
Ministry of Justice, 35–37, 42, 48–49, 105
Montesquieu, Charles De, 54–55

Nationalist Party, 33–34
Nemesis, H. S. S., 28

Opening Up and Reform Policy, 37, 40, 49
opium wars, 28

patent law, 65, 79
Pei, Minxin, 4
People's Republic of China, 4, 13, 35, 60, 62, 65
People's University, 96–101
piracy, 65–66, 68
product safety law, 61–63, 68

Republic of China, 33–35
rice roots lawyers, 43, 46
rights, 9–10, 27, 35, 46, 48–49, 56–57, 61, 65–66, 68–69, 71, 81–83, 98, 123, 130, 144, 160–161
rule of law, 3, 53–55, 59, 88–89, 133
   distinguished from rule of man, 57, 71–74
   formal legality, 4, 55–57, 70–71
   formal theory, 55–57
   governemnt limited by law, 57, 69–70
   history, 79–85
   substantive theory, 56–57

Shakespeare, William, 7
Shanghai, 5, 13, 29, 66, 69, 74, 87, 92, 95–96, 106, 113, 116, 121, 124, 127, 130, 134, 137, 140, 146
Shenzhen, 40, 134–135, 137
sifa kaoshi, 49, 104–105
silk road, 24
Solomon, 97, 99
state legal worker, 39, 41, 46
Strategic Economic Dialogue (SED), 63

Tamanaha, Bryan, 58, 82, 84
Thompson, E. P., 59, 151

Tibet, 70, 104
trademark law, 65, 72, 78–79
Treaty of Nanjing, 28

Washington, George, 22
Wei, Pan, 69
Wen, Jiabao, 12–13
Wu, Yi, 63

Xi, Jinping, 13
Xi'an, 34
Xiaonei, 65, 67
Xinjiang, 104, 160

Zhou, Enlai, 12
Zhu, Yikun, 70

About the Authors

Richard A. Komaiko is the chief executive officer of Leximetrics LLC, a legal-technology-development company. Mr. Komaiko is a former research fellow at the United States–China Economic and Security Review Commission in Washington, DC. Mr. Komaiko has published in the popular and scholarly presses on strategy, economics, and law. He holds a degree in economics from the University of Illinois and has studied Chinese language and culture at the University of Chicago and the Beijing Institute of Education. He speaks English, Mandarin, Spanish, and Hebrew.

Beibei Que is the president of the Chicago chapter of the Chinese American Bar Association. Ms. Que was born and raised in Shanghai. She is a native speaker of Mandarin, Shanghainese, and English, and she is also proficient in French. Ms. Que holds a degree in economics from Illinois Wesleyan University and a JD from the University of Illinois. She is admitted to practice law in Illinois, Pennsylvania, New Jersey, and Washington, DC.